THE VERINDON CONSPIRACY

T0359909

rhiza edge

The Verindon Conspiracy

© Lynne Stringer, 2022

Published by Rhiza Edge, 2022
An imprint of Rhiza Press
PO Box 302,
Chinchilla QLD, 4413
Australia
wombatrhiza.com.au

Cover design by Carmen Dougherty
Layout by Rhiza Press

Print ISBN: 978-1-761110-75-7

A catalogue record for this
book is available from the
National Library of Australia

LYNNE STRINGER

THE VERINDON CONSPIRACY

The Verindon Conspiracy

© Lynne Stringer, 2022

Published by Rhiza Edge, 2022
An imprint of Rhiza Press
PO Box 302,
Chinchilla QLD, 4413
Australia
www.rhizaedge.com.au

Cover design by Carmen Dougherty
Layout by Rhiza Press

Print ISBN: 978-1-761110-75-7

rhiza edge

For my mother, Claire.

For my mother, Claire.

CHAPTER ONE

Misilina stood at the gateway, tensed, ready to spring. The walls on either side slanted in, sealing her in a confining cage. Above her was only darkness.

She barely looked at the warped reflection that shone back at her on the metal wall but noted her dark eyes held intense concentration. She'd confined her hair to a braid to keep it out of her way.

It wouldn't be long now.

A siren sounded and the gate sprang open. She hefted the two blasters—one in each hand—and felt the pulling at her face that meant she was going into the safety zone. She was now in the Vendel safe state where she would be stronger, faster and instinctively know her enemies' moves, but only for ten minspans. Would that be long enough?

A distorted reflection leered back at her from the mirror-like surface of the wall, revealing the change as her jaw elongated and her eyes became empty black sockets with a pinprick of red in the middle. The image was tinged grey, of course, like everything was when she was zonal.

Whispers of danger entered her mind as she crept down the corridor. She knew she had to be fast, but rushing would make her careless.

She felt a flicker of danger above and to her right. It was an englebird, its claws extended, ready to tear her flesh. She aimed both her blasters at it and it vaporised with a shriek of rage.

One enemy down.

The path before her widened out into an open area, although still enclosed with walls. A roar sounded to her left—a parcack. Its claws clattered on the floor, its slobbering, broad mouth dripping saliva as it lumbered towards her.

This shot required more care. Parcacks had few weak spots. She used her safety zone abilities to find the small patch of white on its thigh. She aimed, but it moved too quickly, its claws latching onto one arm. Gritting her teeth, she turned her arm up, bending away from its grip, shooting it in the jaw while targeting the thigh with her other blaster.

It took three shots before the carcass fell to the floor. She didn't bother to check the wound on her forearm.

Then it was down another corridor, this one opening into a forest. It was night, the woods around her filled with dull moans and the shrieks of terrified ransims as they were slaughtered.

A lowan slithered from the undergrowth, its skin shining, its six feet scrambling on the dirt, its lips pulling back in a snarl, revealing the dagger-like teeth behind them.

She darted to the side, using her enhanced speed to get around it, but it snarled again, slamming its front feet down in front of her. She leapt over it, aiming for a kill shot, but the lowan whipped around, its claws tearing at her sleeve as it tried to gain a hold on her.

She jumped over its back again and as she passed over its head, she put one blaster on each side of its neck and fired. The lowan uttered a groan and sank to the ground.

Passing through two marker trees, she sped up. Killing the lowan had taken longer than she'd anticipated.

Rounding another tree, she stepped between two stone pillars and looked at the scene before her. The arena was small and made of large grate rock pieces piled on top of each other. She hefted the blasters and prepared for the onslaught. She had only three minspans left in the zone.

Enemies came from all directions, all off-world creatures, all sentient. The big Garlopagus came charging towards her, its tusks puffing steam. Its crossbow had her in its sights. She leapt to avoid its bolts, rolling under the sweep of its arm, shooting at its chin—its only weak spot.

Diving out from under its falling body, she saw the Trell snatching at her, its brown furred hands grabbing her wrists. It bent her hands back so she couldn't aim her blasters. She lifted a foot and pushed off from its belly, her legs narrowly missing its fangs, and shot it as she turned.

Then there was the Mindalis, its tentacles wrapping around her wrists and her throat. She sank her teeth into one and it released its hold long enough for her to fire her blasters into each of the tentacles wound around her arms. Then she thrust her blaster into the flap on its chest, exploding its heart.

As its tentacles fell away, she turned for the next. A Randoid. Its long arms left a trail in the leaf litter at its feet. The strength in those arms was far greater than hers. It aimed its long-barrelled bolt blaster at her. She dived behind the Mindalis' body, returning fire. But the only way to kill a Randoid outright was a shot straight in its ear canal.

She leapt to the side, her time in the zone just about up, using the last spurt of its energy to hit it precisely in the ear canal. The Randoid thudded to the ground.

She took a breath and looked around. Surely it was dead?

Weapon at the ready, she crept closer. She was a handspan away when the Randoid leapt towards her, grabbing one of her arms. She tried to line her blaster up against its head, but she only had microspans left in the zone …

The Randoid raised its blaster and, with a guffaw, pointed it at her. Her body exploded into flames.

'Damn it!'

The arena faded away, the calm mirrored walls of the training room taking its place. She came out of the safety zone instantly, gasping for breath. She'd pushed it to its limits. Not that it mattered now.

'Student Misilina, your assessment is now complete. Please vacate the training room and rejoin your class.'

Well, that had been a failure. It was a pity this was her final assessment and there'd be no more opportunities to improve her mark, although she knew she'd be able to do some revision before she started working as an agent.

She made her limbs move, even though the loss of sugar in her system made them feel like she was dragging grate rock. Wearily, she opened the door of the training room and stepped into the corridor.

A group of students were already there, some sitting on benches, others gathered around the virtual monitors that screened each student's progress through the simulations. She kept her head down as she headed over to where Enyi sat, ignoring the smattering of applause that sounded from around her.

Enyi's brow was coated with sweat and her lungs were heaving. She lifted her sugar canister to her mouth as she handed one to Misilina.

'Thanks,' she said, hardly able to look at her friend.

But Enyi's dark eyes sought hers out, her sleek ebony eyebrows rising. 'You did so well in there. It was amazing. I couldn't believe the way you killed that Iowan.'

Was she serious? 'Didn't you watch till the end? I was stuck by a *Randoid*, of all things.'

Enyi frowned. 'Randoids are excellent fighters. Strength and skill. And they left it until the end—until everyone was just about exhausted.'

That wasn't an excuse. 'Still ...'

'You know you might never really face one on a mission.'

Misilina wasn't so sure. 'There are plenty of mercenaries out there of all races.' She lifted the sugar drink to her lips and felt strength wash over her, replenishing the sugar in her system that had been drained by the safety zone.

Finishing her drink, Enyi reached for her empty canister. 'Our class is done. Let's go and see how everyone else did.'

The door to the training sector slid open as they approached. Two corridors later, they were in the student room. All fifteen of Misilina's

4

classmates were there, surrounded by lower-level students who had been put through their own assessments, each person's face reflecting their performance, some exulting, some shamefaced, some devastated.

Dehall put her nose in the air at the sight of them, her pinched face cutting a scathing glance. 'Of course, Missy comes floating in ready to lord it over all of us, probably thinking she's scored the highest. Well, you were *second*. Meekan beat you.'

Ignoring her use of that appalling nickname, Misilina reeled in shock. She'd come *second*? Seriously? What had everyone else been doing in there?

But the chorus of approval, some remarks tinged with jealousy, confirmed it.

'She got ninety-five. I was lucky to scrape by with a pass.'

'Meekan was the only other one to take out both the lowan *and* the Mindalis.'

But I bet he killed the Randoid. Never mind. This audience wasn't the one she'd wanted to impress anyway. She let the green-faced looks wash over her, choosing not to respond when asked to critique Meekan's performance. That was their mentor's job, not hers.

And what would he think? Her mentor? The one whose approval she most desired. She knew all too well what *his* result had been when he'd undergone the same assessment during his time at the Academy. Ninety-eight. Why couldn't she have done that too? At least she could count on his help going forward. Together they would correct all the mistakes she'd made.

The door slid open as the new students came in, just coming up from the junior level. Their eyes opened wide as they looked around the study room with its tiered rows of seats. There was an open space at the front for their mentor, who would instruct them from a raised platform complete with a large virtual screen and the latest virtual computer console. There were also assorted weapons—all non-operational so the rookies didn't accidentally kill themselves while they were learning to use them.

She could tell Enyi's youngest sister, Selitian, when she came through the door—same dark face and curly hair, although hers fell to her shoulders. Selitian looked at the platform, the desks and the virtual hangings on the wall depicting different fighting techniques against different species, lists of strategies for many different situations, and the screens that relayed the highlights from their training assessments.

She came to join Enyi, her shining eyes turning up at Misilina. 'I saw how you did in your assessment. I mean … wow. I couldn't believe it. Amazing. I hope I'm that good when I graduate.'

Enyi glared. 'What about me? How did I do?'

Selitian turned to her sister. 'Sorry, you did really well too.'

Her friend folded her arms. 'Thanks for the concession.'

'You lost to the lowan,' Selitian said.

Enyi's eyes flickered to Misilina. 'I still got ninety.'

That wasn't all that surprising. Enyi's skill was in strategy, but it was more on the level of planning a mission, rather than in close combat. Still, Misilina had expected a little higher from her friend. They'd had plenty of training with lowans. Misilina wondered if Enyi would appreciate some revision rounds too.

A voice from the front of the room drew their attention. 'First-years, please take your seats. Final-years, please stand at the back until I dismiss you.'

As their mentor entered, Misilina could hear the gasps of shock from all the first-years. Although most had heard about him, the reaction at the sight of him was always the same. Selitian's eyes became rounder and they swivelled to meet Misilina's.

The girl took in Misilina's features and looked back at their mentor. It was clear she'd noticed what they had in common—the same dark hair, the same eyes. Their height was different, of course, but that was to be expected. Misilina had gotten her height from her mother.

The major difference was in the scars. They ravaged their mentor's face, deep etchings that cut a jagged line down his cheeks, crisscrossing over his nose, and running in rivulets down his neck. But his eyes were still bright, intelligent, all-knowing, unstoppable.

'Welcome to our strategic fighting course,' said Mentor Keridan. He showed no sign that he'd noticed the reaction that rippled through the newbies. 'Here, you will learn more about not only fighting but also what wins fights, missions, wars and battles of all kinds. And that is strategy.

'Some of you watched our final-years going through their assessments just now. What did you see?' As Mentor Keridan spoke, the virtual screen behind him showed highlights from their assessments. Misilina could see herself in the mix—once, twice, then a few more times. Dehall cast an envious glance her way.

But then the image paused on her failure with the Randoid.

'Even our top-tier graduates can occasionally make mistakes,' said Mentor Keridan. 'While Student Misilina's run was exemplary in every other respect, she slipped with the virtual Randoid. Do any of our new students know what she should have done?'

Most of them seemed clueless, but after a hesitant moment, someone spoke up. 'She came in from the wrong direction.'

Mentor Keridan seemed pleased. 'Enlarge on that answer.'

The student, a young boy, stuttered. 'She needed to change the angle when she shot the Randoid. It wasn't at the right angle to penetrate all the way.'

'Exactly,' their mentor continued, as Misilina's face burned in shame. 'Timing is everything in battle, and knowledge of your enemy and how to combat its weaknesses makes all the difference, both in planning and on the field. A famous resident of Lisenus—a planet some of you know as Earth—once said, "know your enemy". The more you learn about each and every race, the more skilled you will be at planning strategy and defeating your opponent in combat. It will become second nature to you. It *must*.'

A couple of rookie girls sitting in the back row, just in front of Misilina, brought their heads together. 'What do we care about some alien from Lisenus?'

'Well, *he* does. His bond-partner's the crossbreed who grew up there.'

This revelation led to a flurry of whispers that Misilina tried not to hear. But their hisses were not lost on someone else. 'Students,' Mentor Keridan snapped.

Both girls looked up, cringing.

'I'm glad you think you don't need to listen to what I'm saying. That means you've volunteered to undertake the first training assessment.'

They glanced at each other, faces paling. 'But Mentor, we can't—'

He pointed at the door, where an aide was standing. She led the trembling girls away.

'Now, I invite you to go and watch their progress,' their mentor said to the remaining first-years. 'Study it, see what could be done better, and what *you* could do better when it's your turn. Dismissed.'

His pronouncement sent a wave of terrified chatter throughout the newbies. Misilina smirked. Mentor Keridan didn't make examples like that every year, and she was glad he had with those two. She wondered if he'd heard what they'd said.

As she and Enyi got up to leave, Dehall gave her a scathing glance. 'So sorry our mentor chose to use your assessment to show everyone what *not* to do.'

Enyi turned Misilina away but another barb from Dehall flew over the crowd towards them. 'And I bet you know *all* about Lisenus, don't you, crossbreed?'

Mentor Keridan looked up from where he was conferring with another aide. The look on his face parted the crowd, leaving nothing to block his glare from hitting Dehall with full force. She quickly slunk away.

As they headed towards the rec room, Selitian joined them. Enyi gave her an irritated look. 'Shouldn't you be reviewing those training assessments as Mentor Keridan told you?'

But she directed her gaze at Misilina. 'It's him, isn't it? He's … You're …'

'Get,' Enyi spat, and Selitian scurried back over to her peers.

Misilina could feel her jaw muscle tightening as Enyi looked back at her. 'Don't let Dehall get to you. It's just because you're better than she is.'

'Misilina!'

They turned to see Mentor Keridan approaching. They stopped in the wide arch that led into the rec room, Enyi smiling at her as she slipped inside, leaving Misilina with her mentor.

She turned to face him, wondering what pronouncement he would give on her performance.

He put his hands on her shoulders. 'I just wanted to let you know how proud I am of you. We always knew Meekan would get the highest mark, but we haven't had two graduates finishing with such high marks in years.'

'Yes, but it was hardly a perfect run though, was it?' She gestured to the room they'd just left, where he'd screened her failure for everyone to see. It was difficult not to react but she couldn't stop herself from turning away, heading for the rec room, dodging the knots of students congratulating each other on results and commiserating others, getting drinks from the servery, engaging in some casual sparring on the comm screen games in the corner.

It was ridiculous, of course. Yes, she'd failed with the Randoid, but she could still improve. There was always room for improvement.

Her mentor followed. 'I included it because it made a good point. And I don't know if you noticed, but we showed all your successful hits too. And you know perfectly well that everyone fails sometimes.'

'You got a higher mark.'

'Higher. Mine wasn't perfect either. And failures still came in missions.' He chuckled. 'Ask your mother about that sometime.'

Yes, she'd heard the stories. Stories of how her parents had met. Stories of how he, Keridan, the stickler for the rules, had broken their greatest one by falling in love with the woman who had been Lady Sarah, the overlord.

It didn't matter that it had all worked out in the end. She didn't care that the rule had only been established because of a mad system of control that had caged their race—the Vendel—rather than allowing them full access to their powers. They'd still had the safety zone, but their ability to cast powerful waves of energy had been deliberately suppressed by their crazy leaders. She still wasn't sure why. Her father said it was because of their hatred of females, but while a female Vendel cast the power, she couldn't even create it without the help of a male—a male she loved. Energy casting came from a bond of love between two agents committed to each other in every way, so why would they ban it? It glorified love over everything.

Maybe the old regime had detested love too.

Fortunately, that was in the past. Their race now allowed love and encouraged agents to bond with those they loved to gain as many energy casting couples as they could. But it had been a different matter when her father had graduated. It had been forbidden to fall in love, and it was completely out of the question for an agent—a Vendel—to love an overlord or anyone from the ruling family, who were all Verindals, the other humanoid species that inhabited their planet.

Her father, one of the greatest agents ever, had broken the rules, risking his life and the life of Lady Sarah. He had been prepared to lose everything just because he had fallen for her.

The *former* Lady Sarah. Her mother. A crossbreed. Someone who had faced death because of what she was. She was the child of an illegal union between a Vendel and a Verindal. Misilina's grandmother—her namesake—had been unfaithful on her bond-partner, Overlord Darnell, the leader of their people, and had conceived her mother with an agent! If the two lovers had been discovered back then, they would have both been executed.

Someone signalled to her father and he stepped away from her. 'Remember, there's no shame in failure if you learn from it.'

She gave him a reassuring smile. She knew that. And she knew he'd help her. She was already planning another session in the virtual training rooms where she would run the assessment again and again and again, as long as it took to get a perfect mark. That was one of the good things about him being her father—she got extra time with him.

She pushed her way through the congratulations that came from all sides before her attention was drawn again by her father's voice, this time for an official announcement, his face beamed onto virtual screens around the room.

'Students, please give me your attention. The judging panel has finished calculating the marks of all graduates. Yours will be sent to your comm units momentarily.'

Before everyone could pull out their units, Mentor Keridan raised his hands. 'I would like to claim your attention, however, for the announcement of this year's medallists.'

Misilina bit the inside of her mouth. *Keep calm!* She couldn't let anyone see her disappointment if she didn't receive one.

'I am pleased to announce that Meekan has earned the medal for fighting, Asalia has earned the medal for piloting, Nessan has won the medal for leadership, and Enyi the medal for strategy. And the all-round agent medal goes to Misilina. Please congratulate the award winners.'

A ripple of applause passed through the room as Misilina allowed a smile. The all-round medal was the one her father had attained, so her heart sang with joy, but she held it in, especially as she saw Dehall's gaze fixed on her. She knew what the girl would be thinking.

Sure enough, it wasn't long before she came over to spit her venom. 'I guess your father had a word to the judges, didn't he, Missy?'

Needling Misilina was bad enough. Questioning her father's integrity was intolerable. She snapped her fist up, ready to smash it into Dehall's face, when a hand grabbed her elbow.

'I'm sure the judges will be so glad to hear that you think they've played favourites,' Misilina's mother said smoothly.

Dehall's eyes flashed fire, but Mother held her gaze, her blue eyes glittering steadily at her opponent. Eventually, the student's face clouded as her bravery dissolved into a pout. 'It was only a joke.'

Mother's mouth formed a thin line. 'I'm sure they'll be relieved to hear it.' Dehall's face paled a little; she knew Mother was a prominent figure in the government. While Misilina doubted her mother would bother their leadership over something so trivial, Dehall didn't know that—her life was littered with trivialities the size of mountains.

With her foe vanquished, Mother turned and drew Misilina into a hug. 'Missy, I'm so proud of you!'

Misilina let the hug hide her face. 'Mother, please don't call me that.'

Her mother drew back, amused guilt crossing her face. 'Oops, sorry. I keep forgetting you're too old for that now.' She drew her arm through hers. 'But I wanted you to know how proud we both are of you. It's so exciting, especially since you got the same award as your dad.'

'Dad?' She knew what it meant, of course, but it sounded strange in Verindonian and it turned heads.

Mother wasn't troubled. 'Just a little Earth colloquialism. You know how it is. None of this "Lisenus" trash for me—it's Earth and always will be.'

Her mother's loyalty to the primitive planet where she'd grown up was okay at home, but in the middle of the rec room, it was way too embarrassing. She hissed at her. 'Mother, not here, please.'

Mother laughed. 'It's a mother's job to embarrass her daughter.' But she lowered her voice before continuing, 'But now you'll have the pleasure of receiving the award from Lord Jolan.'

Oh no. It can't be! Misilina tried not to scowl. 'Not from Overlord Ardon?'

'He's off-world at the moment. Cress went with him; both our ruler and his heir needed to be in attendance. Jolan is standing in.'

Misilina glanced around, hoping no one would notice the look on her face. 'Why Jolan?' Having grown up with all four of the overlord's children, she was as familiar with them as she was with her brothers.

'Tesrin won't be—he's still buried in his studies. Takes after his mom, that one.' Again with the Earth-talk. 'And Tilla's gone to host some celebration.'

Misilina tossed her head. Jolan was the tormentor of her childhood. 'Will his new girl be attending as well?'

Mother's eyes searched her face. She must have picked up her tone. 'I don't know. I guess we'll have to wait and see.'

Yes, they would. Wait and see if he took a bond-partner or if this was just another shiny-eyed, empty-headed courtier he'd discard once he grew tired of her. He seemed more serious about this one, but 'serious' for Jolan meant a few weeks, at best.

CHAPTER TWO

Mother's more nervous than I am.

She should be used to this—the third of three children who had all won medals, but her hands shook as she straightened Misilina's red-gold formal uniform, making sure the sash was laid just right where it crossed her chest and tucked into her belt. 'Mother, it's fine. Stop fussing.'

But there were tears in her eyes. 'Oh, my darling. I'm so proud of you.'

Misilina looked around to see if anyone was watching. The atrium was filled with the families of the medal winners and other mothers and fathers were hugging their own champions.

Her brother David, whose blue eyes and brown hair mirrored Mother's face as he towered above her, chuckled as he drew her away. 'Come on, Mom. It's going to be fine. Misilina knows the drill. She's seen it all before.'

Misilina tried not to screw up her nose at David's casual use of her mother's weird phrases. Her eldest brother often spoke that way, in spite of her telling him how much it annoyed her. She saw the smirk appear as she gave him an irritated glance.

Not that she'd take him on. David had won the medal for fighting; something that had enraged her other brother, Hajitis.

Hajitis stood back, arms folded, watching the fuss. Detached. Aloof. Finally, he pushed himself away from the wall. 'I can't believe you're getting the all-round medal. But I guess that means you weren't the best at anything in particular.'

She knew better than to bite at his jibe and tried to silence him with a look instead. But Mother came to her rescue. 'Would you say the same thing about your father, Hajitis? He won that medal. Given that he was once considered for the position of high commander, I suggest you watch your mouth.'

Hajitis humphed and sauntered away, Mother rolling her eyes at his back. 'Honestly, he's so like his namesake it makes me wonder about the power of a name.'

'The great Agent Hajitis,' Misilina said. Hajitis was a legend amongst their race and had saved both her parents' lives.

David's amused gaze drifted to his brother's retreating form. 'I don't know about that, Mom. After all, I won the medal for fighting. He only scored the leadership gong.'

The what? Misilina shook her head. 'David, can you speak normally, please? Half the time I don't even know what you're talking about.'

'Sorry, sis, but Mom and I understand, don't we?' He drew Mother to his side.

Mother laughed. 'Give your sister a break, at least today.'

He looked shamefaced but the twinkle in his eye belied that. 'I'll go see if they're ready.' He stepped up to the door of the main hall where the ceremony was being held.

No sooner had he gone than Mother started to pluck at Misilina's uniform again. 'It's fine, Mother. Please don't fuss.'

David reappeared, his face surprisingly sombre. 'Um …'

Mother frowned. 'What's wrong?'

He didn't seem to know where to look. 'It … it seems there was a mistake.'

Misilina could feel her face paling. 'What?'

'The results. They got them wrong. I'm sorry, Missy. There's no medal for you.'

She felt her body sway, her world slipping out from under her. This couldn't be real. 'How could that happen?'

But Mother's eyes flashed with lightning. 'David, don't you *dare* do that. Have you no shame?'

To Misilina's relief and anger, he burst out laughing. 'Sorry, Mom. I couldn't resist. It was just another test. It seems Missy still hasn't got it.'

He tried to put his arm around Misilina and she elbowed him in the stomach. She caught the look of surprise on his face as he doubled over. 'That's what you get for lying to me.'

Even then, he couldn't stop himself. 'Hey,' he said, struggling to get his breath back, 'just seeing if you've picked up Mom's talent yet. Guess not.'

Misilina shook with rage. Why couldn't he shut up about that? It was bad enough that he'd pretended she hadn't got a medal after all, but to poke her about that again? No, she wasn't like Mother, who was the most talented lie detector on the planet, something that had caused their scientists a great deal of wonder after they'd discovered her joint parentage.

Identifying lies was a talent possessed by female Verindal in the upper classes. Mother had gained it through her Verindal parent—Misilina's grandmother. Given that Mother's other parent had been a Vendel man, no one could work out why her lie-detecting talent was so extreme. Some thought that the injection of Vendel blood had made it stronger.

But then Misilina had been born and even though her father was a pure-blood Vendel, she had yet to show any ability to identify lies, no matter how blatant they were. She should have started to show a talent for it around her tenth birthday and now she was seventeen, so they'd all but given up hope that it would appear. It was the only thing she'd wanted to inherit from her mother and she hadn't got it.

'By the way,' said David, now his breath was back, 'they're ready for you.'

Mother smoothed her hand once more over Misilina's uniform and pushed her towards the main hall. 'We'll be out front, darling.'

Misilina joined her fellow medallists as they lined up at the connecting door, positioning herself after Enyi. Her award, being the all-round medal, would be presented last. Enyi raised an eyebrow at her, the curve of it meeting the fringe of her curls. 'I guess this is it.'

'Yes,' was all Misilina could think to reply, horrified that her voice sounded shaky. She took a deep breath and calmed herself.

A moment later, the door opened and the five medallists marched through into the main hall. Misilina cast her gaze around the room, which had been draped with multicoloured fabrics that complemented the subtler colours of the walls; a much different look from the Agency main hall in the old days, which had been all white. The new Agency didn't keep a stranglehold on its agents. If it did, she was sure her parents would have moved their family to Lisenus by now.

The hall was filled with family members and other students, faces open and smiling—except the ones who were green with envy—as the five of them took their positions on the stage to the left of the podium where her father stood, ready to address the gathering.

A raised dais was in the centre of the stage with a throne on it. Not the overlord's throne, with its lukis-encrusted engravings over every part, but a smaller one. There were still lukis gems sparkling their colours in the light, even though the person on this throne wasn't as prestigious as the overlord.

Misilina knew Jolan well; after all, they'd effectively grown up together. Mother had never forgotten the debt she owed to Overlord Ardon for saving her life back when things on Verindon had come so close to war. Back when the agents—the Vendel—had practically been slaves, but more enslaved by their own people than by Jolan's race, the Verindal.

When it had been discovered that Mother was the child of a Vendel and a Verindal, it had led to an uprising that had nearly destroyed their planet. Overlord Ardon had helped stabilise the new regime, something that still seemed to surprise Mother since Ardon was about as serious as Jolan. Of course, Father had been there to help rebuild things, settling all the simmering tensions.

Even now, there were still those who whispered that Vendel and Verindal didn't belong together. But Ardon wouldn't listen and had given her mother a prominent position in the government. Her job was to unite both Vendel and Verindal, but she hadn't managed to stop the rumblings of restlessness behind everyone's smiles.

Jolan was the youngest of Ardon and Talma's four children. She'd been chased by him as a child. He'd tickled her mercilessly, annoyed her endlessly and had set her hair on fire. She remembered the smell of flaming hair and the sound of her shrieks as Mother had put the fire out while Father held Jolan by the scruff of his neck and Overlord Ardon rocked with laughter. She felt a haze of anger as she remembered even Father biting back some chuckles as he'd told Jolan off. It had been an accident. Apparently.

All this passed through her mind as she cast her eyes over the throne where Jolan sat. He was dressed in regal splendour—a deep blue tunic, a scarlet cape underlaid with all the colours of the rainbow, as well as darker blue trousers. He looked regal. She wondered if it would last the duration of the ceremony.

Their eyes met and he winked. She quickly looked away. She wondered if his girlfriend was around. Doubtful. Many of the elite Verindals at court still kept their distance from the agents, although Misilina had wondered if curiosity might bring her.

She turned her attention back to the proceedings as Father began speaking.

'Students and graduates, families and friends, welcome to this year's medal ceremony. We're proud of the graduating class this year, as every student has performed to an exceedingly high standard. We're excited at the quality of graduates who will join the Agency's ranks in the year to come.

'As you know, in the years since we rebuilt our society into one unit of people rather than two, no graduate of the Academy has ever been forced to work for the Agency. Other professions and positions are open for selection by any Vendel who seeks them.'

'But they're hardly as prestigious, are they?' said Enyi under her breath.

'In this way, we continue our dedication to a society with freedom of choice available to both Vendel and Verindal.' Keridan smiled down from the lectern as there was a smattering of polite applause. 'We are also honoured to have Lord Jolan here to award these graduates with their medals of distinction.'

After more applause, Jolan pushed himself off his throne and sauntered over to the podium as Father stood aside for him. Running a hand through his light hair, he smiled disarmingly—or impudently, Misilina thought—at the audience.

'Thank you so much, Mentor Keridan, for your kind words.' He grinned and several females in the crowd fluttered their eyes at him. 'I'm delighted to be here in my father's place to present the medals to these distinguished graduates. They're a credit to the Vendel and a great example of the high standard the Agency encourages from all its graduates.'

He was doing okay, but it sounded a little forced. Misilina knew he wasn't overly fond of official events. Hopefully, he wouldn't lower the tone with a wisecrack.

His face seemed bright and alert as he turned towards the five of them. An aide stepped up, holding out a box inlaid with lukis stone. In it were the medals, star-shaped and made from lukis, each with a multicoloured ribbon attached.

Jolan draped one around the neck of each medallist. He smiled at them as he went, although no words were spoken. When he stepped up to Misilina, she could see amusement in his hazel eyes. Had it been there for everyone else or was he just subjecting her to it? She felt her lips press together as he put the ribbon around her neck.

Then he turned back to the gathering. 'Join me in congratulating our medallists.'

As the crowd clapped and cheered, Misilina noticed Jolan's gaze still fixed on her.

***

Before Ardon's rule, no member of the ruling family would have stayed for all the celebrations, not that they'd had many back then. When her mother had ruled, she'd been shocked at how the agents were practically enslaved by their own kind—living and dying ... most dying—taking part in missions that were more about lining the pockets of their leadership than anything else.

But now the celebrations were open for anyone who wanted to attend. And Jolan stayed, the life of the party, entertaining all around him with stories that Misilina didn't get close enough to hear, especially when she noticed the other medallists looking her way and laughing.

What *was* he telling them? Probably all the humiliating stories of a childhood spent trying to steer clear of his antics.

And Jolan hadn't come alone. Of course, he had two agents guarding him—only two, unlike his mother and father who always had five each with them—but he had brought someone else. Judging by the way she was fawning all over him, hanging on his every word, she was his latest girl.

She was beautiful, Misilina had to acknowledge that, but Jolan always attracted the beauties. Being in the line of succession did that. Her long blonde hair was piled up in curls at the top of her head and her sleek gown lined her body so tightly Misilina wondered how she'd managed to squeeze into it. Multicoloured flashes dazzled Misilina's eyes whenever the woman swayed her hips, which was often.

Misilina hadn't expected her to come to the ceremony and she certainly hadn't thought she'd stay this long at an agent-run event. Was there something different about this one?

Jolan took the girl's hand and led her over to Misilina's parents. Misilina slipped closer so she could hear what they said. She could tell Father was on alert—some of the Verindal elite reacted badly to Mother. He would be watching for any sign of that.

'Keridan and Sarah, I would like to introduce you to Mandine,' Jolan said with a smile.

While Mother nodded in greeting, she let Father reply. 'It's nice to meet you. We appreciate you coming to support the graduates tonight. All support and recognition from elite families is welcome.'

Mandine's blue eyes flitted to Mother, but her look seemed more curious than haughty. Then she turned a bright smile on Father. 'Thank you so much, Mentor Keridan. Jolan speaks highly of you and the incredible skill you have in training your students.' Her face faltered a little and she raised a tentative hand towards one of the scars running down Father's left cheek. She didn't touch it, just hovered her hand there. 'Does that hurt?'

Father's face remained smooth. 'It did when it happened, but no longer.'

She nodded, an empty look on her face. 'It must have been so frightening. I've heard all the tales about that terrible day. How awful.'

Misilina knew Mother would see the tiredness in Father's eyes but doubted anyone else would notice. 'We won the day,' Father said. 'That's the most important thing.'

Mother glanced around, probably looking for a distraction, and unfortunately, her eyes landed on Misilina. 'Missy, come and meet Jolan's ... friend.'

Yes, what do we call her? The prospective? The chosen? The latest? There were many things she'd rather do than meet the current decoration hanging off Jolan's arm but she walked forward and forced a smile on her lips.

Mandine's eyes brightened as they fell on her. 'Oh yes. You're Jolan's little childhood friend, aren't you? I've heard all about you.'

I'm sure you have. 'It's nice to meet you,' Misilina said, holding her smile in place. She was an agent now. She could consider this her first mission—remain polite and non-committal to Jolan's ... whatever.

But now Mandine knew who Misilina was, the laughter was clear on her face. 'Oh, Jolan was very wicked to you, wasn't he? He's told me all the stories.'

Mother flinched and Father's eyes darted to Misilina's, but

Jolan wasn't troubled. 'All good ones, of course, Missy. Why would they be anything else?'

'Of course,' Misilina said. Jolan wasn't stupid. Misilina knew he would see the glint in her eyes.

Did he care? No. He continued to grin at Mandine and their eyes caught and held each other's gaze. Eventually, the two of them seemed to remember there were other people in the room and Mandine turned back to Misilina. 'By the way, congratulations on your award.' She gave Father and Mother a nod. 'You must be proud.'

'We are,' Mother said.

'At least,' Mandine continued, 'agents are *allowed* to be happy now. It was terrible, the old ways. We should be grateful they're gone.'

That line sounded so rehearsed. She'd probably heard variations of it from other elites and copied them. Maybe she'd dictated some compliments into her wrist comm before she'd arrived. Misilina could imagine her discreetly holding her wrist up to record the best of them so she could get the words just right.

But was she bright enough for that? Probably not.

Jolan's guards came to his side, whispering in his ear. He turned back to them. 'Duty calls and my schedule for tomorrow is full.' He stood to attention before Father. 'It was an honour to be here for such an auspicious occasion.'

How could he make everything sound like a joke? She didn't know how Father kept serious. But he did. He always did. 'It's an honour to see our ruling family involved.'

Jolan drew Mandine's hand through his arm, smiled at Mother then at Misilina, winking at her when his companion's back was turned.

Mandine was oblivious as she held out a hand to Misilina. 'I'll see you soon, I'm sure.'

Misilina took her flimsy grasp; it would have been rude to do anything else. *I highly doubt it.*

CHAPTER THREE

The celebrations were over and the graduates honoured. Now it was time to get to work.

Misilina was focused as she approached the recruitment office. She was refreshed from the week of leave after finishing her studies and had confirmed with their leadership that she intended to become an agent. She didn't know any graduate who wasn't. And she was ready to see what assignment she would get first.

Enyi fell in step with her as they walked down the corridor. This part of the Agency was still much like it had been in days of old. The walls around them were white and bare, the ceilings releasing a muted glow of light, the floor beneath them smooth and polished by the feet of many an agent who had passed this way for word on their latest mission.

'What do you think we'll get?' Enyi asked, her voice high with excitement. 'Something off-world, maybe?'

That would be sensational, but ... 'I don't think too many graduates get to do that on their first mission these days, even medallists,' Misilina said. 'They usually have to break us in first.'

At least it was unlikely there would be any street duty or clerical assistance. Perhaps a job guarding a member of the high family or shadowing another more experienced agent in some local field mission.

She knew when her father had come through the Agency there had been no gentle introduction to their missions. The agents were thrown into whatever was available. Back then, agents were mostly considered expendable, although medallists had been treated a little better.

Father had been lucky. He'd been enormously talented, and the high commander back then, a man named Denzik, had planned to groom Father to take over when he'd retired. But Father had been less malleable than Denzik had thought and less desirable because of it. It hadn't helped that Father had gone and fallen in love with Mother.

Even though Misilina had trouble admitting it, doing that may well have saved his life and had definitely saved Mother's. It was also largely responsible for the freedoms they now enjoyed. No more were they forced to go on missions with no expectation of returning. No longer were they expected to leave their fellow agents to die rather than jeopardise the success of the mission. Their current high commander, Zaden, treated them all with respect.

But the recruiting room was still sparse and cold when she and Enyi entered. About twenty workers sat behind desks, virtual screens in front of them, feeding information into their terminals, barely glancing at the long line of graduates in front of them, every face eager, but quickly looking crestfallen as each was handed a chip with the details of their assignment.

'I've got to supervise dust sweepers. Since when did they need supervision? Are they doing heists on the side?'

'Keeping the peace on the streets of Underdarton? I've lived there for years. Nothing ever happens!'

'Ugh, mining duty. The lowest of the low.'

The mumbles and grumbles came from all sides until an imperious woman at a slightly raised desk in the middle tapped something on it, three staccato beats ringing out. 'Anyone complaining about their assigned duties will be reassigned to mining force.'

Silence fell. Soon a whisper of complaint was heard again, although it was silenced by another irritated tap. The graduates who had received their assignments hurried to get out of range of her hearing.

Misilina waited patiently until it was her turn to step up to a desk. The man behind it barely glanced at her. 'Name?'

24

'Misilina.'

His eyes turned to hers. 'Misilina, medallist?'

She didn't know any other graduate who shared her name. 'Yes.'

He dropped his gaze back to the screen and pointed to his right. 'Go to the overseer's desk.'

She joined yet another line and waited again. Fortunately, this wait was shorter, as the overseer frequently squinted at the face before her and barked at them to get out of the way. As a result, the line moved steadily as graduates fled the woman's glare and stepped into longer lines. Even Misilina was slightly uncomfortable at the snarls of the overseer as she crept closer, but she kept reminding herself that she was a medallist. That meant something in this place.

Finally, it was her turn. She kept her gaze straight and her voice determined. 'Graduate Misilina.'

The woman looked her up and down. 'Misilina, receiver of the all-round medal?'

'Yes.'

She pointed to the side of the room. 'Stand over there.'

Misilina went to the corner indicated, wondering why she hadn't been given a chip. She wasn't about to plague the woman by asking, though. As the continual parade of graduates marched through, she was joined by her fellow medallists. Eventually, only the five of them were left.

The overseer left her desk and came towards them. She was taller than Misilina had thought, towering over them with a no-nonsense glint in her eyes. *Good. Now we'll get down to business.*

'Follow me,' she snapped. 'Keep your mouths shut.'

She led them through a side door into a corridor Misilina had never seen before. That was saying something, given the prestigious positions both her parents had in the bureaucratic machine. They passed numerous doors on either side of them, but the overseer kept her gaze fixed on the one at the end of the corridor. As she reached it, it slid open and they followed her through.

Misilina recognised the outer chamber of the high commander's suite of offices; its opulence a stark contrast to the bland corridors they'd come through. Warm lights hung in clusters from the ceiling. Each of the four desks in the room was made from real polished wood—no virtual programs. The carpet was a deep blue and the walls a lighter shade. Misilina had been there with Father a couple of times when she was small, riding on his back. She remembered High Commander Zaden tickling her under her chin while she'd giggled. Hopefully, she could shoo away any other embarrassing memories he had of her and replace them with steadfast and capable ones.

Her fellow medallists were agog as they gazed around them. She was sure they knew where they were but doubted any of them had been there before, except maybe Enyi, whose father also worked in the upper ranks of the Agency.

The overseer walked past the four assistants, each seated at one of the desks in the outer chamber. A section of the wall slid back as she approached. The inner room was even more opulent than the outer one, with a shade in every colour of the rainbow, acknowledging and celebrating the beauty of Verindon's multicoloured sky. There were two more desks in this room, and the man and woman seated at them looked up as the overseer approached.

She stopped before the desks, saying nothing. Then, with a wave of her hand, the female assistant set the overseer in motion again, and she marched towards the indigo wall in front of her. A small section slid away and they entered the room beyond.

Only once had Misilina been in High Commander Zaden's private office, and Father had chased her out until he was done. She tried not to look awed at the thick carpet, which contained as many colours as a lukis stone. There was a strong and beautiful real antique desk, with real shelves with real printed books sitting on them. A one-way window ran the full length of the wall, revealing an unobstructed view of their rainbow-coloured sky and a large section of Intersiss, the capital of their planet.

High Commander Zaden rose from his chair as they entered. He had aged in the years since she'd seen him last—there were grey threads in his sandy-coloured hair and care lines under his eyes. But his smile was the same.

'Ah, here are our best and brightest of this year. My apologies for being unable to attend the graduation ceremony to see you awarded your medals, but I had a commitment that couldn't wait. I decided an invitation to hand over your assignments in person was a good way to make up for it.'

He came around the side of the desk and stood in front of them, holding out printed cards. Misilina could see the shock of her fellow medallists. That they should have the honour of receiving their first assignments *on paper* was overwhelming.

Meekan was handed his first. 'You will be assigned to Overlord Ardon's backup guarding squad.' He let out a gasp before High Commander Zaden clarified things. 'Now remember, it's the backup squad. But perform well there, and you will be put on the main squad.'

Meekan worked his jaw before he could get the words out. 'Thank you so much, High Commander.'

Misilina felt her heart flutter. Meekan had been assigned to guard the overlord himself! Even if it was the backup squad it spoke volumes about his capabilities. *What will I get?*

Zaden then offered a card to Asalia. 'Because of your stellar performance in all your piloting modules, you have been assigned to shadow Lady Talma's chief pilot. I hope this will give you a good foundation for future work.'

Yet another assignment for a member of the ruling family. The *consort*, no less!

The high commander then offered Nessan, Enyi and Misilina their cards. 'I'm pleased to say that the three of you will be working together, so to speak. And your first mission will be on Darsair.'

Enyi squeezed Misilina's arm so hard she thought she'd bruise. Their first mission was off-world. She scanned her memory for any political significance to the planet Darsair. It was a small world with some mining colonies, which might be the reason for their mission, as that was an industry Verindon shared. Other than that, it was mainly industrial and didn't have a great deal of prestige. *Why are we going there?*

'I'm pleased to inform you that you, Nessan, will be shadowing Agent Benton as he leads the guarding squad for Lord Jolan. Your leadership skills have led to you shadowing a leading agent on your first mission.' Zaden then turned to Enyi and Misilina. 'Both of you will be members of the guarding squad for Lady Mandine. The two of them are going to Darsair to discuss what aid we can give the Darsairians after a spate of recent mining disasters. It's a goodwill mission.' He smiled.

She could sense Enyi's delight, even as the girl tried to hold it in, but Misilina only felt dismay. She was guarding *Mandine*? That could only mean one thing, and Nessan voiced it. 'I take it this means that Lord Jolan and Lady Mandine are to be bonded, High Commander?'

'They are. The announcement hasn't been made public yet but will be before your departure. Please keep it to yourselves until that time.'

She felt Zaden's eyes pass over her and made an effort to look enthusiastic. But it felt so underwhelming that she was to guard a lower-tier elite female on what was really a show mission and nothing else. She had been asked to babysit a fool. Well, perhaps not a fool, but a shallow elite who probably delighted in nothing more than fancy clothes and waving at crowds. Jolan's other girls had been the same.

She didn't pay much attention to what Zaden said after that, anxious to get away so she could reveal her disappointment only to the mirror. Fortunately, it wasn't long before he dismissed them, but then she had to contend with Enyi's eagerness as they left.

'Can you believe it?' Enyi said, still hanging onto Misilina's arm. 'We're going off-world on our first assignment and guarding the ruling family! Well, we're not specifically guarding a current member, but someone who's soon to join it.'

Nessan fell in beside them. 'I can't remember the last time graduates got to go off-world as part of an elite mission. Definitely not since the great change to the ways of the Agency.' He brushed his fringe out of his eyes and grinned at them, his freckles melding into one another on his cheeks.

Meekan and Asalia joined them. 'We've all got brilliant posts,' Asalia said. 'But you three get to go off-world, and to a planet that's not known for its hospitality. It's the closest the Agency's come to sending new recruits into a danger zone since ...' her faded blue eyes passed over Misilina, 'since your father was leading missions.'

Misilina plastered a smile on her face. 'Yes, it's a great honour.'

Enyi's gaze snapped onto her. 'But you don't exactly seem that excited.'

Misilina needed to try harder. 'I'm just thinking of logistics. Planning things out. You know how it is. There'll be so much to organise.'

'You're right,' said Nessan. 'The three of us should get together and discuss potential situations and outcomes.'

Meekan laughed, his big form huffing. 'Keep in mind that we're all only junior members of these squads. We can plan as much as we like. We'll still have to follow what our *leaders* command. They don't like rookies telling them what to do.'

Nessan's shoulders drooped. 'It doesn't mean we can't try, though. You never know what's going to happen. It wouldn't be the first time that junior agents have been forced to take over a mission because the senior agents became incapacitated.'

Meekan snorted. 'Raw recruits? That hasn't happened for twenty years.'

Even so, Misilina couldn't escape Nessan's plans or Enyi's delight. They assaulted her from both sides as she traded ideas with them and tried to sound enthusiastic.

And she should be, she reminded herself. It *was* an honour to go off-world for her first mission. She shouldn't be so negative about it. It was a tribute to their high achievements in their studies and she needed to treat it as such.

She just wished it wasn't with Mandine.

CHAPTER FOUR

It didn't take long before Misilina appreciated the opportunity she'd been given in going to Darsair. It was a prestigious initial step in her life as an agent. Whatever she did on her first few assignments would form the basis of her future career. Guarding Mandine might not be the most exciting prospect but Nessan was right—getting to go off-world for their first assignment was an honour. She concentrated on that, determined to do everything to the best of her ability.

Mother was delighted by the news. 'It's a fantastic position to get this early in your career,' she said as they watched a vid on the comm channels of Lord Jolan and Lady Mandine announcing their upcoming bonding. 'I must confess I'm surprised at Jolan, though. I didn't think he'd settle down so quickly.'

'His father didn't order it?' David asked, leaning back as he played flick-the-remling on a virtual screen. The scuttling rodents went from one side to the other in front of him, increasing to the thousands, as he used brainwaves to try and stop them.

'I can't see why. He's the youngest. They would be more interested in seeing Cress settle down, seeing as he's the heir to the throne.'

'Too intent on his studies, I think,' said Misilina.

'When do you leave, Missy?' Mother asked.

Misilina managed to refrain from flinching as her mother used her nickname. 'In fifty-four maxispans.'

'That's two days, Mother,' David called out.

Mother scowled. 'Yes, thank you, David. I've lived on this planet for over twenty years now. I know how long a day is here and how long a maxispan is, and I know how long it takes our planet to go around our sun. Lay off.'

She stood behind Misilina as the vidscreen dissolved into nothing. 'Don't worry, sweetheart. You'll do fine.'

Misilina wasn't worried at all, and Mother should have realised that by now. But David gave her a sly look. 'I reckon she's just pining over Jolan.'

'That's ridiculous,' Misilina snapped.

'David,' Mother cautioned.

'Oh, come on, she used to flutter her eyes at him all the time.'

'When I was seven!' Misilina turned her back on her brother.

But he laughed. 'Watch it, little sister. Don't forget that Mom can tell when you're lying.'

'David, that's enough,' said Mother, glaring at him. 'And for the record, I didn't sense a lie in what your sister said, so grow up.'

But although David kept his mouth shut when he was within Mother's range of hearing, the moment she'd gone, he bent over to Misilina with a conspiratorial whisper. 'Mandine can tell when people are lying too, so I'd watch it on the mission if I were you. If you try and steal her man ...'

Experience had taught her that David wanted her to bite. So she collected herself and walked away, leaving her brother pouting behind her.

***

Despite Mother's excitement, Father was the one who escorted her to the loading bay when it was time to leave for her mission. It was better to have his stoicism. It helped her focus.

'Remember all you've learnt,' he said. 'Look and listen. Think all the time. Try and be a step ahead of everything. Follow your leader's instructions, but don't be afraid to speak up if you have an idea and especially if you see something that concerns you. Darsair has a good degree of security in place for this visit, but there can be problems anywhere and with anything. And always trust your instincts.'

She smiled up at him, watching the scars on his face pull as he grinned back and kissed her forehead. 'Off you go. You'll do fine.'

He handed her the small backpack that was standard issue on these assignments. It contained nothing but a few personal effects and her comm unit. She could always produce a virtual version of anything else she needed. All her clothes would be created by the program in her comm unit.

She met Enyi as they headed down the gangway towards the loading bay. The girl gave Misilina a nervous smile.

Misilina ran her eyes over the vehicle before them. It was a new model Star Runner Mark 50. She had only seen vids of one so far. David and Hajitis had discussed it at length with Father. High-rated shielding, swivel guns in five different locations, hyperspeed and alterspeed capabilities. While it was unlikely any of those things would be required on this mission, she knew that no member of the high family would be allowed to leave the planet in anything less.

'Well, this is it. Have you met Agent Tenya yet?' said Enyi.

'No, not yet.' Tenya was the leader of the five-person guard that had been assigned to Lady Mandine. Misilina had quizzed Father about her, but he'd been non-committal.

Enyi gulped. 'She's not exactly friendly.'

'She's not meant to be our friend.' Tenya was the leader of their part of the mission. Their job was to learn from her. That was all.

'Yeah, but we're working under her instruction for at least the next week. It would be nice if she was approachable.'

Misilina gave her a tight smile. 'We listen. We learn. What else is there?'

That earned a sigh from her companion. 'I think you two will get on fine.'

She saw Enyi pull up as a woman approached them, coming out of Star Runner's hold. Her dark hair was pinned back in a severe knot and her eyes were small, her mouth hard.

Her gait was unhurried but determined as she strode up to them. 'Graduates Enyi and Misilina?'

'Yes, agent,' the two of them chorused.

Misilina didn't react as the woman looked her up and down with critical eyes. 'You're almost late. I suggest you come on board.' She turned on her heel and marched back the way she had come.

That assessment sent Misilina's blood pumping. She was *never* late. There were still a good ten minspans before they were due to be there. But there was no point debating it with a woman who was to be her leader, so she followed her without comment. Enyi was a step behind.

Entering the ship's hold via the gangplank, Misilina smelled the distinctive fresh-off-the-line smell of a top-tier Star Runner. All the surfaces gleamed and sparkled, the fittings new and spotless. She followed Tenya down the corridor to the main rec room where there were two more women, as well as Nessan, Agent Benton and three other males, clearly the other members of the squad to guard Jolan.

Misilina had seen Agent Benton before. He had worked closely with Father for a while on some training modules for students at the Academy. He seemed just as calm as he had then, his steel-coloured hair just as neat and unruffled, his grey eyes passive, although Misilina knew that exterior hid an effective and dangerous agent. He could fight with the best of them when he was pushed and had put many a student through their fighting drills in the training rooms. The other three male agents she didn't know, nor did she know the two other female agents. She waited quietly for introductions or instructions.

Enyi was less restrained. 'Hello,' she said, with smiles all around. 'It's great to be working with you.' She glanced at Nessan for support, but he offered a tiny smile and maintained his silence. Knowing how talkative he could be, Misilina couldn't imagine he would be so overawed as to shut his mouth, so presumed he had been ordered to keep silent.

Agent Tenya turned her stern gaze on Enyi. 'Agent Enyi, this is not a pleasure vessel. Save your salutations for a more appropriate moment, not when you're about to be briefed on your mission.'

Enyi swallowed her smile and turned anxious eyes to Misilina. Tenya glared at her—challenging Misilina to speak, she believed. But she maintained her silence and thought she might have seen the recognition of kinship in the older woman's eyes.

Once Enyi was silent, Tenya nodded to Agent Benton, who turned to them. 'Agents Nessan, Enyi and Misilina,' he said, 'welcome to your first mission. We're sure you've realised the high level of trust that has been given to you, seeing that your first mission is primarily off-world. I hope you have studied Darsair extensively so there will be no surprises for you when we're there. Agent Nessan, can you tell me how their government functions?'

There was only a moment of hesitation before Nessan answered, 'It has the perception of a democracy, but systemic corruption means it doesn't always function effectively.'

'Good.' Agent Benton nodded approvingly. 'While many efforts have been made to overcome the corruption on Darsair, there are still some problems in that area. Agent Enyi, can you tell me the different products Darsair mines?'

'Um,' Enyi still seemed rattled by Agent Tenya's rebuke, 'metals and precious stones primarily.'

'Such as?'

'Clandeck, grate and ore rock, and also a gem called crysallin, which is similar to a lukis stone but not as colourful.'

'Well done,' said Agent Benton, to Enyi's clear relief. 'And Agent Misilina, can you tell me what your primary function is on this mission?'

It was a letdown that Misilina received the most basic question, not one that related to all the research she'd done on Darsair. 'The male agents present are a guarding squad tasked with keeping Lord Jolan safe during his visit. The females present are tasked with keeping Lady Mandine safe.'

'What are the dangers that you might anticipate?'

That was a more informative question. 'The possibility of

demonstrations or attacks from those who lost loved ones during the recent mining disasters. Also, there is an element on the planet that seeks to embarrass the government, bringing them into disrepute. Then there are the miners themselves, who want better safety conditions, as well as some former workers who are trying to obtain a more lucrative payout. Generally speaking.'

Agent Benton's eyebrows rose further the longer she'd talked. 'Thank you, agent. I see you have your father's eye for detail.'

Misilina tried to quell her delight at his words so she didn't miss any part of their briefing, but she could feel a cold eye from Enyi.

'Now,' continued Agent Benton, 'here are your fellow squad members.' He nodded to the three men lolling on the couches in the rec room. They didn't do anything more than nod as the graduates' gazes fell on them. 'These are Agents Lerrick, Juvid and Gellar. All three are third-year agents and will also be responsible for flying us to Darsair. Agent Tenya, would you care to introduce the rest of your squad?'

Tenya barely spared a glance for the two women who sat quietly but attentively. 'These are Agents Amatara and Dina. They are both second-years, although they've both had extensive field experience.' She waved her hand dismissively at them. 'That is the end of the briefing at this time. Further information will be given once we are on our way. You may now introduce yourselves informally as Agent Benton and I rendezvous with the royal couple.'

She left without a backward glance, Benton giving them a polite nod as he departed.

Once they'd gone, Enyi and Nessan seemed to breathe easier. Nessan started chatting to the other members of his squad and Enyi smiled at Amatara and Dina. 'So you're second-years? How did the first year go?'

Amatara didn't seem inclined to reply, keeping sullen green eyes on her comm unit, using her auburn hair to hide her face from them, but Dina smiled at them. 'My first few missions were short and uneventful, but I spent the second half of the last year on Tarden helping a peacekeeping force there.'

Misilina nodded. 'Tarden has had a great deal of civil unrest for the past eleven years, hasn't it? Where were you stationed?'

Dina's short golden hair shone in the light as she cocked her head at Misilina. 'You're a mine of useful information, aren't you? I was stationed at their headquarters. It wasn't arduous work, as it was probably the safest place to be, but then, I was only a first-year.'

'But you received the medal for fighting last year.'

Dina chuckled. 'Right again. That's why they let me go to Tarden.'

Amatara's eyes slid in her direction. 'What did you do wrong?'

Dina frowned. 'Wrong?'

'Yes, you were given a prime posting last year.' Amatara's piercing gaze bored into her. 'Now you're babysitting a spoilt elite.'

Dina's look could have drilled holes in Amatara. 'Guarding an elite is important work.'

Amatara snorted and Dina raised an eyebrow. 'Well, maybe when Tenya returns you can tell her this assignment is beneath you and see the response you get.'

The two of them sat with their backs to each other after that, Amatara refusing to enter the conversation. Misilina didn't say much. She was too busy listening.

'Agent Tenya seems … intense,' Enyi said.

Dina smirked. 'Isn't she? Highly talented, I hear. I haven't worked with her before but one of my associates from last year said she was the most regulated agent she'd ever met. Never steps out of line, never breaks the rules, doesn't think much of agents who do.' Her gaze fell on Misilina. 'She doesn't think much of your father.'

Misilina could feel her face paling. 'What?'

'He broke the rules back when they counted, fell in love with the overlord, no less. She hates that.'

What does that woman know about Father? 'I guess it's her problem if she hates a talented agent.'

A shrill voice came from the gangway. Tenya reappeared, looking like she'd just been dragged through a hatch of parcacks. 'Agents, you are required to line up on the gangway, the males on the right and the females on the left.'

She didn't wait to see if her orders were obeyed and everyone scrambled to their feet, heading out as quickly as they could. Nessan took his place at the end of the line behind Lerrick, Juvid and Gellar, and Enyi and Misilina let Amatara and Dina go ahead of them. They positioned themselves behind Tenya, who stood at the bottom of the ramp.

Agent Benton approached, walking beside Lord Jolan, who caught Misilina's eye and grinned. She looked away quickly, hoping her fellow agents hadn't seen that. She hoped no one would think it indicated any partiality towards her.

The gabbling came from Mandine, who was talking nonstop to a portly man at her side. Misilina had seen Councillor Veston before she'd realised that Mandine was his daughter. He owned some low-grade mines, which he'd tried to trade for a lukis mine a few years earlier. The deal had fallen flat and the gossip about it had been immense, even amongst students at the Academy.

Looking at him now, no one would have guessed he had any troubles. He simpered and smiled at Jolan but barely spared a glance for the gathered agents.

Another woman trailed in their wake. She carried several bags, two gripped in her hands with another tucked under each arm. She moved quickly and quietly behind Mandine. Of course. She would be Mandine's lady-in-waiting. Misilina wondered if Mandine had had her for long. Some elite women had their own lady-in-waiting, but unless they were members of the high family, usually they didn't have more than one. Mandine would have to wait until she and Jolan had bonded before she had a chance of gaining any additional ladies. Most women in the high family had three. And of course, Mandine wouldn't be expected to wear virtual clothes, hence the heavy bags the poor girl lugged along.

As they reached the Star Runner, Agent Benton stopped and directed the elites towards the gangplank as the agents bowed. 'My Lords and my Lady, these are the agents who have been assigned as your guarding squads while we're on Darsair. I will be leading Lord Jolan's squad. Lerrick is my second, and we will also be supported by Juvid, Gellar and Nessan.'

Jolan was generous with his smiles. 'I'm sure they'll prove themselves in short order, agent.' He looked at Nessan. 'You were a medallist this year, weren't you?'

Nessan flushed as he was singled out. 'Yes, my Lord. I won the medal for leadership.'

'I'm sure you'll learn a great deal from such experienced agents as Benton and Lerrick.'

Jolan had inherited his ability to compliment from his mother and his inability to take anything seriously from his father. Even as he spoke, Misilina could see a familiar light of mischief in his eyes. Did he mean what he said? Possibly. She'd given up trying to work it out.

As Benton fell silent, Tenya stepped forward and offered her own bow. 'My Lords and my Lady, I will be leading Lady Mandine's squad. I will be assisted by Dina, who is my second. We will also be supported by Amatara, Enyi and Misilina.'

Mandine smiled at them but turned her head as her lady-in-waiting proceeded up the gangway with her possessions. 'Be careful with those, Keily,' she scolded. 'They're the important things.' She glanced behind her, and only then did Misilina see three more servants pushing several large trunks up the ramp and into the hold. One of the metallic trunks bumped into the wall as it was wheeled along, letting out a clang. Mandine didn't flinch as Keily returned to her side. 'Make sure everything is stored properly in my quarters.'

'Yes, my Lady,' the girl said. She seemed young for her position but didn't seem overawed by it if her bored expression was anything to go by. Her almond eyes took everything in calmly, her short dark hair framing her face.

Jolan gave the female agents a wide smile. 'A soon-to-be bond-partner has so many things to worry about.' Again, his eyes fell on Misilina. She hoped he wouldn't wink at her.

Fortunately, he nodded to all of them. 'Fine-looking agents, one and all. One medallist from last year and two from this year amongst them.' He took Mandine's hand. 'You'll be well-protected, darling.'

Mandine finally managed to direct her attention to the squad of agents. 'I'm sure they'll do well.' Her smile was as vacant as her eyes.

Veston passed his eyes over them. 'Two from this year, you say?'

'Yes, my Lord,' said Tenya. 'Agent Enyi won the medal for strategy and Agent Misilina won the all-round medal.'

The councillor nodded his greying head. 'Strategy, yes. That's useful. All-round agent, was it?' He eyed Misilina. 'She didn't do well enough in anything to stand out, I take it?'

Misilina barely managed to control her face. The fact that she did was a miracle, especially since everyone else, even Tenya, gaped at him in amazement. The only one truly undisturbed by his pronouncement was Mandine, who fixed a cold eye on Misilina. Gone was any of the friendliness she'd offered at the graduation party. As Misilina had thought, that had just been for show. Now Mandine treated the agents as Misilina had always expected her to. The way most of the older elite did—like they were servants.

Jolan was still smiling. The expression looked fastened to his face. 'Actually, Councillor, I believe it means she excelled at everything.'

Veston's smile seemed more of a smirk. 'Really? Well, that's fascinating.' He held out his arm to his daughter. 'Shall we, my dear?'

The two of them proceeded up the gangway and into the hold of the ship, Mandine chattering to her father. Misilina looked at the other agents, all of whom avoided her gaze. Still stinging from her humiliation, she didn't look at Jolan but could feel his eyes on her. If only Tenya would dismiss them!

Tenya's mouth twisted as she spoke. 'Agents, please ready for departure. While we're in transit to Darsair, you won't be required to shadow your charges but you will still be under their command for the duration of our journey. I don't believe you will be needed much, so take this opportunity to settle into your quarters. We shall launch in a maxispan. I expect you all back in the hold by then.'

Misilina kept her head down as she hurried inside, but she was halted by a hand on her arm.

It was Jolan. She kept her face serene as she raised her gaze to his and noticed his expression was pensive. 'He didn't mean it, Missy. He just didn't think. You know what the elite are like.'

He was trying to make her feel better. But if she had truly controlled her face, he wouldn't have realised she was upset. She couldn't be upset over such a little thing. 'I understand completely, my Lord.' She ducked her head in a bow and stepped away from him. 'You should go first.'

She didn't understand the look he gave her. Considering he'd just been trying to comfort her—sort of—she had expected sympathy in his eyes or perhaps merriment, given who he was, but instead, there seemed to be something else.

After a whispered word to Tenya and Benton, Jolan headed inside. They followed him.

As Jolan disappeared, the two senior agents strolled towards the hold. They must have forgotten she was there. 'And we have to put up with that for the whole assignment,' Benton grumbled.

'Only the daughter,' Tenya reminded him. 'At least half the stupid will be gone. Imagine if we had to guard them both.'

Their whispered words were clearly not meant for her ears so Misilina slunk away towards her quarters, still trying to forget what the councillor had said. But it haunted her at the launch and continued to plague her every time she looked at Mandine.

CHAPTER FIVE

Tenya was right—they were rarely required during the six maxispans it took to fly to Darsair. Mandine spent most of her time in her quarters. They could hear her voice from the rec room as she alternated between gushing with excitement and berating her lady-in-waiting.

Jolan spent most of that time in the hold chatting with the agents, almost as if he wanted to get to know them. Misilina cringed in embarrassment, though, when his talk turned to their childhood.

'Of course, I've known Missy for years,' he announced. 'We used to play together in the palace grounds all the time.'

Agent Benton glanced at her. 'Missy?'

'Sure. That's what we called her. Misilina took too long to say.'

Misilina felt her back stiffen and kept her eyes down to avoid the gazes she could feel on her. Did he have to do that?

Annoyingly, Jolan didn't seem to realise what he was doing. *It's my first mission and he's talking nicknames and games in the garden! Could things get any worse?* At least Mandine wasn't there to deride her. That was something.

When they reached orbit around Darsair, they had to wait a maxispan before the Tekkon docking station could clear them for landing. Misilina took advantage of the time to refine her list of the challenges of the planet, hoping local security was seeing to things like the unrest amongst the miners, as there were only ten of them to guard both Jolan and Mandine, as well as the lady-in-waiting. At least Mandine only had one attendant and Jolan none. Agent Benton was prepping him on the journey and, when they got there, he would be assisted by the Verindonian ambassador, who had been in residence in Tekkon for several months.

As they prepared to land, Mandine and her lady-in-waiting appeared. Mandine was wearing a skirt and a blouse, both loud with colour. Her lady-in-waiting fussed a bit with one sleeve, which looked perfectly fine to Misilina. Eventually, Mandine slapped her hand away.

The lady-in-waiting, Keily, sat next to Misilina. She didn't seem troubled by her boss's rebuke. She sat demurely, looking around her, glancing at Mandine every time she spoke.

Enyi turned to Keily. 'Enjoying your job?'

There was a barb in her words, but Keily didn't seem to notice. 'It was nice of my Lady to take me on.'

Enyi frowned. 'Is this your first job as a lady-in-waiting?'

'Yes. My family are miners. We'd fallen upon hard times. My Lady runs some charities in the mining sector and she heard of our plight and came to the rescue.'

Misilina had heard about Mandine's charitable interests. A lot of elite females had them. For most, it was just a front to make them look good while they let more capable individuals do all the work. Did this mean Mandine actually *involved* herself in her own charities? That was a surprise.

Keily's eyes fixed on her. 'You're the crossbreed, aren't you?'

Misilina kept calm. It was hardly the first time that question had been thrown at her. 'My mother is half-Vendel and half-Verindal, yes.'

Her reply was a little terser than she'd intended but there was no indication that Keily noticed. 'More Verindal than Vendel, I heard.'

That was unusual. If Keily was from a mining family, then she was a Verindal. Usually, if a race pointed out that Mother was a crossbreed, they wanted to disown her, so would automatically classify her as a member of the other race. 'More Vendel, actually.' It was a common misconception. Mother's cells had originally favoured her Verindal side but had been rewritten the first time she'd gone into the safety zone. Now they favoured her Vendel side. She wasn't going to waste time explaining that to Keily.

Still the questions came. 'But she can still identify lies?'

'Most definitely.' It was Mother's strongest ability.

'But you cannot.'

'Apparently not.'

That made Mandine lift her head. 'Yes, poor little Missy. The only thing worthwhile to get from her mother and she missed out.'

Misilina resisted the urge to defend her mother. They shouldn't be sticking their noses in her family's business.

Jolan shifted in his chair. 'I think there's a great deal of good to get from Ambassador Sarah, actually. There's no one as skilled as she is at keeping peace between our two races, and in interplanetary relationships as well.'

Keily fell silent and Mandine huffed before rearranging her face into a pert smile. 'Yes, she's been a great help in keeping our races united.'

How much longer until we land?

Finally, the Star Runner left orbit and headed in, landing at a large docking station in the middle of the city. Misilina peered through a window on the side of the ship for a glimpse at an alien planet.

The first thing that struck her was the absence of colour. Father had warned her about that. 'You'll want a rainbow sky. You'll want colour on the ground, colour in their dress, colour in their decorations. It will be the most immediate loss.'

He was right. Their sky was a washed-out red, their sun a dull orange. The clouds were grey and only seemed to make the surface of the planet darker. In fact, most of what she could see was grey tinged with red—there were few plants of any kind within sight, most areas paved over. As far as she could see there were dull-looking buildings of different sizes, some with colourful lights in their windows, but the overall impression was drab.

As they came closer to the city of Tekkon, she could see some statues and engravings on every building—squat, angular creatures. At least the port they were approaching looked clean and new. It was a few spans from a prominent set of buildings that resembled block upon block of grate rock, except they seemed to be made of metal if the way they caught the light was anything to go by. From what she had gathered in her intel, this was the headquarters of the Tekkon government.

Agent Tenya appeared, directing her stern gaze on Misilina. 'Enough sightseeing, agent. Come and take your place.'

She opened her mouth to tell Tenya she'd been simply getting the lay of the land but thought the better of it. She doubted her superior would enjoy being lectured like that.

So it was back to the rec room where Mandine was preening herself in front of the full-length virtual mirror Keily had created from her wrist comm. Jolan's head was bent close to Agent Benton, receiving final instructions.

'Ambassador Utreysin will greet us, my Lord,' Benton said. 'He will take you to Tekkon headquarters first and will fill you in on your schedule while we're here.' He glanced at Mandine. 'I believe there's a dinner tonight in honour of your visit.'

This made Jolan's bride-to-be prick up her ears. She nodded at her lady-in-waiting. 'Make sure my best evening gown is ready. We must make a good first impression.'

As the Star Runner docked and the three third-year agents did final checks before opening the gangway, the five female agents positioned themselves around Mandine. Tenya was at point, Enyi and Misilina behind her, on either side of Mandine, with Amatara and Dina behind them. Once Jolan's squad joined them, Misilina noticed that Nessan was put in the same position as her around Jolan. It must be the position assigned to the least experienced agents.

Misilina checked that her comm unit was set for weapon function, even though it was unlikely it would be needed when they were disembarking. She gazed reassuringly at the three cans of liquid sugar fixed to her belt. The belt straps were standard issue on their jumpsuits and they checked the canisters daily. Without them, they would lose their ability to go into the safety zone.

As the gangway thudded to the ground, Jolan made his way down, his guard around him, and Mandine followed, her lady-in-waiting bringing up the rear behind the teams.

A corpulent Verindonian approached with his arms spread wide, his bloated face grinning with pleasure as he bowed low. 'Ah, Lord Jolan. What an honour it is to greet you on your first visit to Darsair.'

'Thank you, Ambassador Utreysin,' Jolan said. 'I'm happy to be here on behalf of Overlord Ardon.' He waited for Mandine to come to his side, the agents parting to allow it, reforming around the two of them. 'This is my soon-to-be bond-partner, Lady Mandine.'

Again the ambassador bowed, his girth almost touching the ground. 'Indeed. Such a privilege to meet so beautiful a lady.'

Mandine smiled archly at him. 'Thank you so much.' She looked away from him before she'd even finished speaking, taking in her surroundings. 'What an interesting place.' But she screwed up her nose and raised the hem of her skirt off the ground.

Misilina looked around them. It was a standard docking station, large and sprawling, with many landing bays leading off it on several levels. While it wasn't prestigious, the bay they'd been assigned was clean and serviceable. Mandine's behaviour was nothing short of rude, especially considering this was an official visit.

Ambassador Utreysin saw it too and took the hint. 'Please, come with me and I'll take you to Tekkon headquarters where your chambers are located. I'm sure you'll be pleased with them. Only the best will do for visitors from Verindon's high family.'

After Jolan's guard had entrusted the Star Runner to the care of a Tekkon ground crew, they were ushered into ground vehicles—rollers—that were plush and comfortable. They were big enough that all five members of the squads and their charge could fit in with ease. Utreysin took a third vehicle, which he begrudgingly shared with

Keily and Mandine's luggage.

Misilina scanned the surroundings as they sped along on the surface of the roads. She'd known that Darsair's streets were on the ground—they didn't use fliers as their primary transport as they did on Verindon—and after she got over the strange vibration caused by the hover engines pushing against the road, she appreciated the insight it gave her into the streets around them. She realised the docking station was much larger than she'd first thought, perhaps containing three hundred landing bays. It wasn't bad for a planet of this level. She chided herself for not checking the station's specs before they'd arrived. She'd have to make sure she did so in the next few days. It was useful information and she should have thought of cataloguing it earlier.

The streets they raced through were devoid of other traffic, probably because they were using them. She saw some other rollers being held at intersections by Tekkon's crowd control, the force that kept peace in the city.

Most of the buildings they passed were grey and made of metal. It looked fairly low-grade, although metals weren't her specialty. They seemed well-constructed, clean and new, perhaps evidence of Tekkon's recent upgrades to try and appease the various groups that objected to the government's treatment of the miners.

They approached a larger construction with many of the statues she'd seen from the Star Runner. It was closed off—they were waved through by the guard at the gate.

They drove into a covered area under the nearest building, where there was a disembarking station. The five of them jumped out. Keily raced up to take Mandine's hand and help her out, but she was quickly replaced by Utreysin. 'This way, my Lady.'

Jolan and his squad joined them as they headed inside.

Here, their surroundings were brighter. Tuneless music tinkled in the background and the walls on either side of them were covered with angular shapes that they were told represented Tekkon's governors.

Misilina could see Jolan and the ambassador engaged in quiet conversation. She wished she could hear them, hoping to get some understanding of any potential dangers they might face. However, she had to settle for guard duty, although the corridor was empty, so it was hardly a hotbed of dangerous activity.

They went up several levels before the ambassador stopped at a door and bowed. 'Lady Mandine, this is your suite of rooms.' The door slid open to reveal a bright sitting room, walls splashed with colour, plush carpets under their feet, couches dotted around. Another door on the other side was bound to lead to the lady's bedchamber.

At a nod from Tenya, all of them took prearranged places around the sitting room as Mandine sashayed in. There were two attendants, both Verindal, waiting there to greet her, and she sat immediately, allowing them to ply her with food—Verindonian, of course—clearly designed to tempt a fussy elite.

Misilina looked at her leader, but Tenya had stationed herself closest to Mandine. Surely they needed to be briefed on their roles at the dinner? Apparently not. Tenya stood vigilantly not far from Mandine as the woman let her attendants gush all over her, telling her how beautiful she was, talking about her gowns and the latest fashion on Verindon.

But a bold little attendant leant forward. 'You know, my Lady, you'll need to be careful tonight.'

Misilina tried not to show her interest, but every facet of her being was focused on what the attendant was about to say.

'The governor's wife dresses in splendour herself and doesn't like to be outshone. However, I know that the governor detests her and will probably be pleased if you make her look as dour and old as possible.'

Mandine glanced at her lady-in-waiting. 'I don't imagine that will be a problem. I doubt Darsair style will come close to anything we've brought with us.'

'But you must be careful, my Lady,' said the attendant, 'not to outshine her too much. We must keep relations with the Darsairians cordial.'

Mandine waved a dismissive hand. 'If her own bond-partner doesn't care for her, why should I?'

Misilina looked away, crestfallen. Were they really going to discuss nothing greater than scoring political points through the quality of their garments? She reminded herself what she was there for—to guard Mandine. That was all. But how could she do that if she didn't know the latest intel on security? They needed to be updated on any new threats.

She looked again at Agent Tenya. She was calm and unruffled. She was an experienced agent. She would discover what intel they needed and her subordinates would be told at the time. Until then, she could only do her job.

But at that moment, her job was staring around the room, ensuring safety. And how could that be compromised when the most dangerous creature in sight was a shallow aristocrat?

***

The ambassador's dinner was unremarkable. Misilina spent the evening shadowing Mandine with the rest of her squad, listening to the never-ending hum of conversation.

She kept her mind alert by watching the Darsairians and cataloguing the differences between them and her people. The room was the first thing she'd noticed. She'd heard that the Darsairians favoured block design and, sure enough, the room was a perfect square, the seating padded blocks of varying height and length, the artwork cubes upon rectangles. There were some colourful drapes on the wall, but when Ambassador Utreysin gave them an approving look, Misilina surmised that they must be his doing.

She turned back to Mandine, who stood with the governor's bond-partner. True to what they'd been told, the woman was dressed gloriously, but the riot of colour on her dress with its triangular shapes was so bright Misilina felt like shielding her eyes. Mandine's nose remained tilted up the whole time she spoke to her, clearly glorying in the shimmering gown she was wearing and striking poses that seemed designed to show it to its full effect.

Misilina watched to ensure that the governor's bond-partner showed no sign of aggression, nor did any other Darsarians. They were a strange species. Their bodies gave an angular impression, with square shoulders and wide hips. Even their heads had something angular about them, although they still could have passed for a Verindonian to a casual observer.

'I'm *so* happy to be here with Lord Jolan,' Mandine said into the comm unit that Keily held out for her. 'We'll do all we can to support your people after your recent mine … problems.'

Misilina listened as the comm unit translated Mandine's sentence into Darsarian. Fortunately, the program chose a restrained Darsairian word. If Mandine had called it a catastrophe, the translation would have been much more extreme. As it was, the Darsairian noblewoman simply bowed and smiled, putting her fists together in front of her—a Darsarian show of respect and welcome. The translator bud on her throat spoke out clearly. 'We will be grateful for any and all help from Verindon.'

Mandine smiled and looked at Jolan as if seeking an escape, but he was conferring with Tekkon's governor, serious looks on their faces. It was not an expression Misilina was accustomed to seeing on Jolan.

Mandine excused herself to go and get some refreshments from a nearby table, all five of them, and Keily, going with her. She picked through the jellies and treats, which were all cube-shaped, with disdain. 'Angles, angles everywhere,' she snipped. 'Don't these people know how to curve?' She ran a hand along her hip as she said it, fluttering her eyelashes and laughing.

Keep your mind on your job. Misilina wasn't sure whether she'd thought that at herself or Mandine.

The elite waved a hand towards Tenya. 'One of you agents might know the answer to this. I asked Keily but she was clueless. Why do they have throat translators and we have to rely on our wrist or hand comms?'

'Verindon is investigating the throat technology, my Lady,' Tenya replied. 'It's relatively new and there have been some problems with it. Also, some consider it unsightly.'

That made sense to the elite. 'There is that consideration, certainly. But why can't we use the chip in our brains? We're given these chips shortly after birth and all they do is relay messages from people and a bit of information here and there. Why can't they do something clever like translate languages? Maybe we could even learn to speak these languages because the chips do the work for us, you know, make our mouths move the right way. Surely that could work?'

Tenya's lips formed a smile but she seemed to struggle to hold it there. 'There have been a great many issues with increasing the use of the brain chips, my Lady. It would be useful if they could download large amounts of information straight into our brains in different forms of teaching, such as languages, but we have found this has caused too many problems for the user.'

Tenya was downplaying it by a long way. The truth was, it had killed some and caused insanity in others. Many Verindonians considered the chips an extreme danger and wanted them removed, or at least, no longer used. This was common knowledge on Verindon. Mandine should have known.

Mandine yawned. 'It doesn't say much, though, for our scientific minds if they can't overcome the problem.' Popping a cubed morsel into her mouth, she turned back to the gathering, smiling vacantly at any Darsairian who peered at her. 'How much longer can this thing go on? You'd think they'd have at least arranged some entertainment for us.'

Misilina hoped Tenya wouldn't object to her speaking up. 'They don't have a lot of entertainment on Darsair, my Lady, not at government events anyway.'

Tenya gave her a sharp look but Mandine seemed more surprised that she'd spoken. 'Yes, but we do. Surely in the name of good interplanetary relations they could make an effort.'

Mandine wandered back to Jolan, perched on his arm, and

chattered away to the Darsairian governor, shimmying around so her gown caught the light. The governor's eyes were drawn to her body, much to the clear dismay of his bond-partner.

And still, her five agents stood nearby, watching for trouble, with Jolan's guarding squad also keeping an eye out. Ambassador Utreysin nodded and whispered occasional instructions to Jolan while Keily kept Mandine supplied with refreshments.

Misilina suppressed a sigh. How many days before they went home?

***

It was the same the next day and the next—nothing but a procession of parties and assemblies full of people occasionally talking about something interesting like local politics, but usually keeping conversation to gowns and parties and likes and dislikes.

'Whoever thought that visiting another planet could be so dull?' Enyi commented to Misilina one evening after Mandine had retired and they were given a rare break. Even then, they weren't allowed to go outside the Tekkon government complex. They had gone up to the roof—a flat top on the highest level in their headquarters.

'That's enough, agent,' came Tenya's voice from behind them. But even she looked weary as she stood beside them, gazing out at the Tekkon skyline. It was an uninspiring sight with its bronze night sky and angular constructions. Smoke could be seen curling up from industrial sites and the breeze brought the faint whiff of sickly-sweet perfume from the crysallin mine on the city's outskirts.

'Are we required, agent?' Misilina asked. Perhaps there had been a development, something that required them to do actual work rather than standing around scanning crowds and getting sore feet.

Tenya's smile seemed almost fond. 'Not for the kind of work I'm sure you'd like to be doing. However, there is the possibility of some tomorrow.'

Enyi's eyes brightened. 'Really?'

'Yes, we're moving the mine visit forward. There have been

rumours of unrest in some circles and the Tekkon government's crowd control thinks it would be better to schedule it before some unpopular measures they're presenting in the next few days.'

That woke Misilina up. 'It's not a good idea to change plans so abruptly. That's when mistakes are made.'

Tenya's eyes flashed. 'Thank you, agent. I am aware of that.'

That's right. Tenya's not lacking in experience. The agent continued to glare at Misilina. 'I'm sorry, I'm just concerned—'

'I know,' Tenya snapped. Then the anger on her face faded. 'We're not happy with the change. We suggested cancelling, but Lord Jolan is insisting we go. He wants to see the progress that the Darsairian government says has been made on safety.

'We will need to be on guard. Even though we've seen evidence of the government's inroads to meeting the miners' demands for better pay and conditions, there have been whispers that the government is taking Verindon's aid and using it to line their own pockets. If the miners believe we're complicit in this, Lord Jolan and Lady Mandine may be targets.'

'So Lady Mandine's going as well?' Misilina asked. She was surprised she had agreed to it. Maybe she had finally tired of being feted and adored.

Apparently not. 'I believe Lord Jolan has cajoled her into going,' Tenya said. 'Whatever the case, she has agreed to it.'

Enyi blew out a breath. 'So not only could there be trouble, but we'll be dealing with a bad-tempered elite as well.'

Tenya scowled. 'That is not your concern, agent.' But her voice lacked its usual vigour. 'We'll do our part and, in a few more days, we'll return home and you will have successfully completed your first assignment.'

With that, she left and they resumed their silent contemplation of the night sky. But Enyi wasn't one for silence. 'Do you think it will be as easy as all that?'

Misilina shrugged. As she'd said, mistakes were made when plans changed abruptly, but … 'Let's hope so. It's been okay up to now.'

'But that's been inside the walls of the government's headquarters, the most well-guarded, fortified place here. Could a bunch of discontented miners break in here? But out there on the streets …' Enyi's eyes shone with glee. 'I could go a couple of rounds with an enemy right now.'

Misilina kept her cool, but her blood surged at the thought. 'Well, you never know. Maybe tomorrow we'll *really* get our first assignment.'

CHAPTER SIX

They were in the same formation as always as they headed to the allocated transports—Tenya at point, Misilina and Enyi next, Amatara and Dina behind them. Lord Jolan's squad was situated around him as well as they headed for one transport, while Mandine and her squad headed for the other.

Mandine tsked as the door of the roller was opened for her. 'Why don't they have fliers? You'd think Darsair would be less backwards by now.'

Misilina saw Tenya check that no Darsairian looked shocked. There were a few locals who could speak Verindonian. Fortunately, those helping them smiled benignly and nodded, thankfully clueless about the fact that their Verindonian visitor was insulting them.

The rollers blew clouds of dust beneath them as the hover engines held them a few handspans off the ground. Misilina took in everything she could about their transport, which seated three of them across, with the other three facing them, their backs to where they were going. Tenya and Dina took their places on either side of Mandine, with Amatara, Enyi and Misilina facing them. Keily was forced to sit in the front next to their driver.

Jolan's roller led the way and the procession travelled swiftly. Misilina noted how their surroundings became more unkempt the further they went. It seemed that only the streets immediately surrounding the headquarters had been renovated and improved. Misilina had pored over every piece of information she could find on Tekkon and the improvements the government was supposed to have made. Fortunately, she'd also looked at all the details of what the city had been like before the changes. She was starting to think that information would be more accurate so began running through everything she could remember.

The rectangular street paving was uneven, the businesses dilapidated and the locals gave them resentful looks as they passed. Their expressions seemed set in a scowl that looked at home on their faces.

At least no one pelted their vehicles with anything. She could see the other agents digesting everything and all of them sat up straighter—more vigilant. They were heading into trouble. Misilina could feel her awareness increasing as her heartbeat sped up. Her mind cleared as she used the focusing techniques they'd been taught in the Academy. It was the first time she'd ever used them in a real situation and she was surprised at how much more aware they made her feel. Anything would be a help.

As they travelled to the edge of the city, Darsair's sun began to set. Days lasted only about six or so maxispans on this planet, and Misilina was unsettled as she watched the light dim. It would have been better to go in the daytime but the Tekkon government had been hard-pressed to get everything ready on time as it was. She craned her neck to see the mine shaft they were approaching, jutting like a gigantic hook out of the ground. Some officials and security personnel were milling around, all wearing grim smiles. The area in front of the shaft had a raised dais with an amplification device set up in front of it.

Mandine frowned. 'Is Jolan making a speech? I didn't know that.' She pouted. 'Nobody briefs me on these things.'

Something fluttered inside Misilina, some feeling of unease. Perhaps Mandine's indignant expression was wearing on her nerves. She looked at Tenya. Their leader didn't seem surprised so it was likely no one had thought Mandine needed to know. *They probably told her and she was too absorbed in organising her garments to remember.*

There was an open area around the dais. The Darsairian officials were waiting for them there. The area was swept and neat, and a gold-coloured carpet had been laid. Beyond this circle of order and calm, there were steel barriers lined by Tekkon crowd control, who stood almost side by side, occasionally buffeted as the barriers were pushed by the many miners behind them.

These miners didn't just wear customary scowls. Each face was dark with anger and they were growling in discontent. It was a wonder they hadn't stormed the barriers, but their shoves seemed half-hearted. Misilina hoped that meant that, for all their ferocious expressions, they weren't given to rebellious outbursts.

Both rollers slowed and stopped. Jolan's halted at the edge of the carpet while theirs hummed behind it, waiting for its turn. His guarding squad came out first—all more alert than she'd seen them since they'd arrived on Darsair. Agent Benton's eyes were everywhere. He made a commanding presence as his gaze pierced the gathered throng. Mutterings sounded from behind the barrier but lessened as his eyes settled there. Even Nessan looked menacing, although Misilina could see how pale he was, his fingers curled reassuringly around the three cans of sugar attached to his belt, probably drawing comfort from the strength he knew they would give him if he had to go into the safety zone.

Mandine seemed oblivious to anything amiss. She smoothed out her dress and looked impatiently at the roller in front of them. 'They're taking long enough.'

Finally, their roller moved forward and all five of them sprang out, Mandine's lady-in-waiting leaping out as well, holding out a hand to Mandine and helping her position her dress so it fell just so. Misilina only gave this scant notice, her eyes drawn to the throng as she heard curses and catcalls at the sign of the wealth Mandine wore like a cowl.

Misilina wondered at the wisdom of bringing any royal Verindonian to this place. While there was no doubt each squad of agents could defeat common folk like this, there were so many of them.

If they decided to attack, the chances of victory were slim. Surely if Overlord Ardon had realised the potential danger, he would have sent them with multiple guarding squads. Why had they come with so little protection? And why, having spent the last few days in the safety of the government buildings, had they gone there?

The Darsairian welcoming committee was all smiles as they bowed before Lord Jolan and Lady Mandine, the Governor of Tekkon stepping onto the podium with a flourishing gesture of welcome as though he was addressing a crowd flushed with adoration. His throat communicator translated his words into Verindonian for them.

'People of Tekkon and Darsairians from all corners, we welcome you here on his auspicious day. We thank you for coming and thank Lord Jolan and Lady Mandine from Verindon for their aid and counsel at this time, as we try and rebuild a mining industry that encompasses all in the region of safety.'

A rumble ran throughout the crowd and Misilina looked at Jolan. For once, his face seemed serious, the smile painted there clearly held in place only by monumental effort. She tried to recall the last time she'd seen him look uneasy. Nothing came to mind.

The governor seemed unconcerned. 'The new equipment purchased from Verindon will, I'm sure, prove effective in helping improve conditions in the mines, as well as increasing productivity—'

'Can anything improve conditions when so many have died?' came a voice from the crowd, speaking in Darsairian. Misilina knew enough of it to translate without the aid of a device.

The governor's flow of words stuttered. 'A productivity that will benefit all—'

'Ha! You mean you fat creatures in your high towers!'

The governor's face faltered. 'And that will help ensure the best outcome for us all.'

'When have you ever considered the people? Why would you start now?'

There were a few more calls but Misilina could only translate one speaker at a time. But did she need to hear the details? She gripped her comm unit tighter, feeling it hum as the weapon function waited for the slightest pressure.

The governor's words dried up. 'I would like to ask Lord Jolan of Verindon to say a few words.'

Misilina cast her eyes over Jolan's squad. They should be calling the roller and getting them back to safety.

But as Agent Benton's head bent towards Jolan, she saw the agent's face darken. Jolan went past him and headed for the dais. Every one of Jolan's guarding squad followed him, their hands on their comm units, ready for trouble.

Jolan's smile was unconcerned but Misilina could see his hand shake as he put his comm watch up to his mouth so that his words would translate into Darsarian. She knew he could speak some of the language already, but he mustn't have felt comfortable trying it at a public event like this. 'Thank you, Governor D'sallo of Tekkon. It's an honour to be here and to know that we can assist your people in making the mines more secure. Verindon has had mines for as long as our people can remember and we pride ourselves on our safety record.

'There is much we've been able to do to assist the Darsairian government in improving their mines, both in structure and equipment, that will go a long way to making them safer and more lucrative for both the workers and those who benefit from what the mines bring forth, which is, of course, something of value for every citizen of Darsair ...'

As he continued, Jolan seemed to relax. Misilina eyed the crowd, uncertain where her gaze should be directed—where the people were the loudest or where suspicious silence reigned? Or would the danger come from somewhere else?

Even Mandine seemed to have realised that there was trouble, beginning to fidget. Her head dipped towards Agent Tenya. 'How much longer is he going to speak?' Misilina heard her whisper. 'There's a dinner later tonight I need to prepare for.'

She could see Tenya steel her expression before muttering a non-committal reply.

The blast sounded so suddenly that it made her leap, moving towards Mandine, as all five of the guarding squad surrounded her.

As screams erupted, Misilina's eyes were drawn to Jolan where he lay on the dais, Agent Benton's lifeless body draped over him.

Tenya raced towards him. 'Quick! Get my Lady back to the roller!' She forced her way through the dignitaries as the frantic crowd burst through the barriers.

'Death to the oppressors! Death to the Verindonian enablers!'

All four of Jolan's remaining squad dived on him, all in the safety zone, pulling Agent Benton's body away, trying to help their charge to his feet. But as they moved him off the dais, Lerrick fell. A few more steps and Juvin and Gellar were taken out, even as they used their enhanced abilities to try and find the threat. Nessan's face, with the sunken eyes and dropped jaw of the safety zone, revealed no emotion as he also fell, lifeless, at Jolan's feet.

Before Nessan's body hit the ground, Tenya reached Jolan. 'Get my Lady to the transport,' she yelled at Misilina and Enyi, signalling for Amatara and Dina to join her. They surrounded Jolan, forming a shield, and managed to reach some of the mining machinery, ducking behind it.

Mandine began shrieking. 'What about me? You're to guard *me*!' She looked frantically at Enyi and Misilina. 'Quickly, get me out of here!'

They tried to battle their way through the crowds to the rollers, but the people pushed back, some running for their lives as shots continued to rain down on them, others producing rods and bashing everyone in sight. Mandine screamed as some men appeared before her, worker's tools raised, ready to cut her down. But Misilina and Enyi used their safety zone abilities to dodge the strikes and their lasers took the miners down quickly.

'The roller!' Enyi yelled, her voice sounding far away, as all voices did when Misilina was in the zone. With Enyi on one side and Misilina on the other, they dragged Mandine through the crowd and threw her in the back of the vehicle. Misilina dived in next to her, pushing the elite down so her head was below the level of the window. Enyi got behind the wheel.

'Head for Lord Jolan!' Misilina said.

That didn't please Mandine. 'Are you crazy? They're shooting at him!'

Fortunately, Enyi didn't listen to her. Jolan was the son of the overlord and he was in imminent danger. His own squad was dead, so he was now their priority.

People scattered left and right as the roller charged between them, heading for Jolan's hiding place. Tenya, Dina and Amatara were all crouched there with him, leaping up every so often to fire their own shots.

'Where do you think the shooter is?' asked Enyi.

Misilina scanned the structures around them and saw a flash of light blast out from one. 'On that craggy outcrop, just to the left of the mine shaft.'

The other three agents had also located the danger and fired towards it, but their weapons weren't as effective at that distance. The roller pulled up at their hiding place and Jolan was bundled in.

'Get my Lord and Lady out of here!' Tenya commanded. 'We'll see to the sniper!'

Enyi nodded and turned around, weaving through what was left of the crowd and dodging scattered bodies. But the shots followed them. Misilina could see Enyi's knuckles whiten as she tightened her grip on the steering column, using her safety zone abilities to veer left or right, letting her instincts help her avoid the shots.

But they had been in the safety zone too long. Misilina could feel her change melting away, and the sweat pouring off Enyi's face told the same story. A moment later, Enyi was forced out of the zone and desperately reached for a can of liquid sugar to replenish, but not in time to dodge the sniper. A blast rang out, taking half the roof of the roller with it, and Enyi's body slumped over the controls.

The roller veered wildly as Misilina dived forwards to grab the steering column. She was forced out of the zone herself and guzzled a drink with one hand, driving with the other, trying to push Enyi's body out of the way with her shoulder. Her stomach jumped into her throat as she felt the vehicle charge down an embankment and she fought to regain control.

Jolan reached over beside her, trying to help, his head bobbing up through the hole in the roof.

'Keep your head down, my Lord!' Misilina yelled, pushing him away, as the safety zone settled over her again. She pulled herself into the front of the roller, managing to steer while pressed up against Enyi's still form. There were trees and old pieces of machinery dotting the steep hillside and only the safety zone kept Misilina from slamming into something.

They levelled out at the bottom of the hill on a deserted road. The slope they'd descended was on one side, with a small field ending in what looked like another steep drop on the other.

It was only then that she realised Mandine was screaming, 'Stop! Stop!'

Terrified that Jolan had been hit, Misilina screeched to halt behind what looked like an old hole driller that had crashed into a large boulder. At least it was cover. Still in the safety zone, she turned to check on the two of them.

Mandine's eyes were wide with terror and her breath came in loud gasps. Jolan was white and as Misilina turned to face him, he leaned forward and grasped her shoulders. 'Are you all right?'

Realising that they were both unharmed and knowing that she needed to recharge, she came out of the zone and drank a can of sugar. 'Yes, I'm fine. What about you?'

Jolan held up his sleeve to reveal two scorch marks from the blaster shots. Another was on the side of his tunic. Misilina reached for it. Was he injured?

But no, he stuck his finger through another hole there, revealing a minor burn mark on his side. 'That's the worst I got, thanks to the agents.'

Yes, thanks to the agents, his guarding squad, who were now all dead, including Nessan, her fellow graduate.

Mandine was still blubbing and Jolan put his arms around her. 'Darling, are you all right?'

'All right?' she shrieked. '*All right*? None of us is all right! Does she even know where we are? We need to get back.'

But Misilina paid no more attention to her as she turned to Enyi's body. Her eyes were still open, her hand empty, and her discarded sugar canister lay on the floor, its contents creating a dark pool around it.

Misilina's eyes stung and she found it hard to swallow. Over the sound of Mandine's sobs, she heard Jolan's soft voice. 'Missy, are you okay?'

No emotion. I can't show any emotion. This can't affect me. I'm an agent. It didn't matter that the new Agency didn't restrict emotions, she couldn't let herself feel anything. She couldn't break down. She would be ineffective. *I've been trained for all circumstances. This shouldn't be a problem.* But she trembled all over as she exited the vehicle, took hold of Enyi's form and dragged her outside, lying her on the side of the road.

She had died instantly; that was clear, mainly because part of her skull had been blown away. Misilina knelt beside her, telling herself to get back up. Jolan joined her there, despite Mandine's protests. 'We'll take her back with us,' he said. 'We can see that she's buried with honours.'

Misilina closed her eyes. 'We can't.'

She could hear his puzzlement. 'Why not?'

'Where would we put her? There's no hold in the back. And the roller needs to be as light as possible. We'll go faster that way.'

When she was certain she was under control, she opened her eyes to meet Jolan's amazed gaze. 'You can't be serious. She was your friend.'

'And you are my assignment. Or at least, *she* is.' She nodded her head at Mandine. 'You now too, of course, since your squad was killed.' She stood up. 'Your safety must take priority.'

'That's the first thing you've said I agree with,' said Mandine. 'Now get back in this vehicle and get us back to Tekkon's headquarters.'

Jolan spun and looked at her with disgust. She blinked up at him. 'Darling, I'm sorry, but we need to get somewhere safe. They can come and pick up the agent's body. The sooner we get back and tell them where she is, the sooner it will happen.'

Weighing her words, he looked back at the front of the roller, then at Misilina. 'Can you drive that thing?'

'It doesn't seem too hard,' she said, 'and we've been out here in the open too long as it is. Quickly, get back in the roller. We need to go.'

But there was one more thing she needed to do before she left. She knelt again beside Enyi.

Standard agent protocol number sixty-nine—if an agent is killed in the line of duty, commandeer their sugar canisters to boost your supply.

It had seemed so rational when she'd read it during training, but she felt heartless as she removed the remaining two canisters from Enyi's belt and added them to the one she had. Now she had three and her friend had none. But Enyi didn't need them and Misilina did.

As she got into the driver's seat, she felt Jolan's eyes on her again and hoped he wouldn't notice she was choking back bile.

CHAPTER SEVEN

Misilina sat still in the driver's seat, running through protocols, searching for all the connections she needed to make. It was so hard when all she could think about were Nessan and Enyi lying lifeless on the ground.

But she had to get over it. She was an agent now. She had to consider what actions were necessary in this kind of situation. She'd been through a million scenarios when she was at the Academy. She knew the Agency code of conduct off by heart. What did it say?

Her mind was so fractured. A screaming elite in the back seat didn't help.

'We need to get back to Tekkon headquarters right now. We can't just sit out here where anyone can find us. Come on. Are crossbreeds brain-dead? Plan us a route back.' She raised her wrist comm, pathfinder selected and at the ready.

Misilina slammed her hand over it, perhaps pinching the spoilt elite's wrist a little too hard. 'We can't just contact them. There's every reason to believe that Jolan was the target of what happened back there. If whoever tried to kill him is determined to, they may be able to pinpoint our location and get to us first.'

Mandine drew breath and opened her mouth in a snarl that quickly faded as a light of realisation hit her face. She scowled instead. 'So we're just going to sit out here? We can't do that. Surely you can drive us back to the headquarters without a pathfinder.'

'Agency protocols state clearly that when junior agents are charged with the safety of any civilians or dignitaries, they need to hold them in a safe location until the senior agent contacts them.'

'You call this a safe location?' Mandine glanced around them. 'We're not all that far away. Rebels could come pouring down that slope any time.'

Misilina's hands flexed around the steering column. 'Agency protocols dic—'

'I don't care about Agency protocols!' Mandine screamed.

Finally, Jolan spoke. 'Mandine, I don't think you're helping. Let Missy work—'

'You want to leave all the decision-making to her? She's just a kid. She knows nothing about any of this. You're the highest-ranking person here. You need to order her to go back.'

Fortunately, he was having none of it. 'She's in charge of our security. She's been trained for this. We need to let her do what she needs to do.'

'Which is just sit here and wait until they catch up to us?'

Misilina couldn't look at Jolan but heard his frustrated sigh. 'Missy, do you really think we should stay here?'

She tried to keep her voice level. 'Protocol dictates—'

'Forget about protocol!' snapped Mandine.

'*Stop*!' Jolan growled. 'What exactly does protocol say?'

At least that was a question she could answer. And already had. 'As I said, we need to wait in a safe location until we're contacted by the senior agent.'

'And what if all the senior agents are dead?' Mandine demanded.

She couldn't bear thinking about that. Jolan hissed something under his breath at the stubborn elite beside him. *Elite!* She barely deserved the title.

There was a contingency for that as well. 'If no senior agent makes contact within three maxispans, the most senior agent present decides on the best course of action.'

'Great.' Misilina could almost hear Mandine's eyes rolling. 'So we just sit out here in the middle of nowhere, waiting for those miners to find us? Do you really think we're safe here?'

'We are at the moment.' It was so hard for Misilina to keep her temper in check.

'Mandine does have a point, Missy,' Jolan said. 'I'm not sure this is the safest location. After all, it's not that far from where we were. There's no doubt that reaching a Tekkon crowd control force or something like that is safer than being out here. Shouldn't we at least try to get a little closer to the city, somewhere we're not so isolated?'

She struggled to hold her head up. It wanted to fall into her hands. What should she do? Jolan was right—it wasn't that far away from the point of escalation. What if her actions left them vulnerable to attack? Should she try to find help?

'I *could* try to find a route that takes us closer to the city centre.' It would be easy enough to program her comm unit with a suitable route, but if it was easy for her, that meant it was easy for anyone else as well. Yet another thing to take into consideration! She needed another plan, something that wasn't the most logical conclusion. That would keep the enemy guessing.

The sniper seemed to be deliberately targeting Jolan. Even if they'd simply been trying to cause mayhem or spark a revolution, he would likely still be a prime target. Whoever had organised this would probably delight in dragging his body through the streets of Tekkon or even having him executed publicly. And even if they'd targeted him only because he happened to be the most prominent person there, that didn't mean they wouldn't still like to make an example of him. A motley group of rioting miners could cause just as much damage as the sniper if they made a concerted effort to kill him as some kind of macabre, delusional retribution.

She started up the hover engines to Mandine's murmur of satisfaction. Jolan jumped into the seat beside her. 'My Lord, you need to stay in the back. It's safer.'

'No. You need help. I'm staying here.'

She sighed but relented. She could hardly order him, at least, not unless his life was in imminent danger. 'Check the dashboard,' she said.

'Look for anything like a pathfinder. It might be safer to use the device here than the ones on our comms.' Might was the operative word, though. Could she take the risk? This was a government-owned roller. They must have tracking on it. Surely they would be able to identify its whereabouts.

But wasn't that a good thing? That meant the Tekkon government would be the ones who found them first. And perhaps they'd be the only ones. Surely their system would be difficult to break into.

Father's words came back to her. *Never assume. Never take the easy route. Never accept that what is most likely to happen will happen. Prepare for every contingency.*

With that in mind, did she dare use a pathfinder on this vehicle even if they could find one? Even then, she would need to circle their destination as widely as possible, coming in gradually only as each area looked safe. Hopefully, they would find a crowd control force quickly. She plotted some routes in her head from what she could remember from her research. Unfortunately, the city of Tekkon was not laid out in a grid pattern. No route back would be easy. And all went through heavily populated areas full of murderous miners who had scores to settle.

Mandine eventually grew impatient. 'What about your safety zone thing? Doesn't it give you things like directions and safe routes?'

Misilina kept her tone level. 'It can, my Lady, yes, but it's for when I need enhanced strength and speed, not while I'm trying to conserve my powers in order to get us back safely.'

'But you have plenty of sugar now,' she said. 'Surely you can spare some.'

'My Lady, if the worst happens, I can only be in the zone for ten minspans without replenishment. I have three cans, which gives me a maximum of forty minspans in the zone. Think about what it might cost to get through a crowd of demonstrators or a riot. I need to save everything in case it's necessary.'

She humphed. 'I still don't see why you can't spare one just to help us find our way.'

Jolan was less patient than Misilina, which surprised her. 'I think you'd better let Missy make those decisions, Mandine.'

'Well, clearly I have to, don't I?' his bride-to-be snapped back.

Misilina drove over a rise, hoping nothing lethal was on the other side. She sighed with relief as she saw some familiar buildings. 'That's the outskirts of Tekkon.'

The other two sat back in their seats and Misilina ran through all the protocols she needed to follow. She kept listening for her comm unit to sound in her mind, signalling an incoming message, but there was nothing. Surely it wouldn't be long. Maybe Tenya was waiting for instructions from Verindon? She had to still be alive. Probably Dina and Amatara as well. They couldn't all be …

No, she wasn't going to think about that.

Yes, Tenya would contact Verindon. They would send replacement agents and reinforcements.

Her musings were broken as she turned a corner to see an angry mob. They were waving diggers and shovels, dancing around another roller they had tipped over and set on fire. As one, they turned at the sound of their engine and rushed at them.

Misilina was in the zone before she could blink, throwing the roller in reverse but keeping her eyes on those in front of them, allowing the safety zone to help her steer the vehicle accurately. Within ten microspans, she had cleared enough space to turn around and race back the way they'd come. No, not exactly that way. But the crowd followed them, roaring in anger. She put her foot to the floor and left them behind.

Once the road was again quiet and dark, she came out of the zone and had another drink. Two cans left. They had to get back before she ran out of sugar.

Mandine was sobbing again. 'You idiot! You should have pushed through them instead of turning around. Now we're further away!'

'Don't be ridiculous,' barked Jolan. 'You saw what they were doing. How could we get through that?'

'Well, what's her safety zone thing for if not for getting through difficult situations?' Mandine spat back at him. 'These agents are useless!'

Was that sound Jolan grinding his teeth? 'Five of them died trying to keep me safe. Remember that.'

'Yes, but you're not safe, are you?' It looked like she was going to continue her tirade but stopped as Misilina pulled over. 'What are you doing?'

'I'm going to do what I should have done from the start. Follow protocol.'

Mandine threw her hands up. 'So we're just back to waiting out here? With that mob coming?'

Misilina groaned. Why couldn't they just follow protocol? If she had, she wouldn't have run into those miners. But it had to have been a maxispan now and she wasn't sure where was safe.

She pulled out her comm unit. There was no help for it. She had to send a message. She switched it to Verindon devices only and put the highest levels of protection she could on it. It shouldn't be received by anyone but another agent. She didn't dare extend it so it reached Verindon. That would be like a shining beacon saying, 'Here we are!'

She put her finger on the screen and opened her mind. *Both Lord Jolan and Lady Mandine are safe but vulnerable. Use message coordinates to confirm location.* She tried to smile at them. 'I've sent a message on my comm unit.'

Mandine pursed her lips. 'I thought you said that was a bad idea.'

Misilina had done so well at keeping her patience in every scenario at the Academy. 'Because I can't see any other way. All routes take too long and involve driving through hostile territory. I'm not sure here is safe either.' *Especially with only me to defend you.* She didn't add that aloud. It sounded too defeatist.

She scanned their surroundings. 'There's a small structure over there. I think it would be better to shelter there in case a hostile arrives first.'

Manoeuvring the roller off the road, she drove through a field, pulling up at the small shack. She put the vehicle on the far side of it, out of sight. Jumping out, she pulled open the shack's rusty and primitive metal door and looked inside. There was some old equipment rotting away, possibly from one of the mines. It was difficult to work out what it had been used for. Most of it was metal boxes, some with wheels, some with cables or pipes curling away, all smelling musty.

Mandine screwed up her nose as she stepped inside. 'We're waiting in here. Perfect.'

You can always wait on the road if you like. Misilina clamped her mouth shut. Lady Mandine's protection was her responsibility. She had to ensure she stayed safe. It was hard to imagine a more challenging assignment.

Jolan said nothing. He didn't look at his future bond-partner but took her hand and led her over to a corner. Misilina made sure they were settled before heading for the window. It was made of a transparent metal similar to the type they used to build their mining hovers at home. She rubbed it with her sleeve, trying to clear away smudges to give her a better view. If trouble did come, it would be difficult for them to get away, as their assailant would be tracking their position via Misilina's comm unit and she couldn't leave it behind. She needed to ensure that Tenya and the others had some way to contact her.

She mentioned this to Jolan and he took off his wrist communicator. 'Could we move the homing signal from your comm unit to this and leave it on the road?'

Why hadn't she thought of that? 'But that will leave you without a communication device, my Lord.'

He shrugged. 'It only works over short distances on Darsair anyway. And if you've got one and Mandine too ... I don't think we'll be splitting up, do you? Two between three will be enough.'

She took his device and attached the tracker to it, then hurried out to the road, placing it in the middle, before jogging back to the shack. She went to the wall on the far side of it, which was, fortunately, made of crumbing pieces of rock. She removed a couple of blocks, making a hole big enough for them to crawl through.

'If an enemy comes, we need to get into the vehicle as quickly as possible,' she said. 'It will be the fastest way to put some distance between us and them. If I signal you, crawl through here and climb into the roller. Stay as low as you can. I'll get us out of here.'

Misilina returned to her post by the window, comm unit in hand, weapon function on. She fingered the two sugar canisters at her belt. Hopefully, she wouldn't need one. Hopefully, the Verindonian ambassador's force would come and rescue them, probably with Tenya, Dina and Amatara in tow. Then they would be taken back to Tekkon and go home.

Would they pick up Enyi's body on the way? Misilina hated the thought of her lying out in the open, where any predator might gnaw on her. Not to mention Jolan's squad. What would happen to their bodies? Would the Darsairians bother to collect them?

They waited at least a maxispan, with Jolan occasionally talking in a low voice to Mandine; trying to comfort her, Misilina thought. Then she heard a whisper of sound and signalled for quiet.

Footsteps. But so faint … Her heart sank. If they were being rescued, there would be more than one. And if they were being attacked by an angry horde of rebels, they would hardly think to be stealthy.

Misilina peered through the window. A lone figure had stopped in the middle of the road and picked up Jolan's device. Even though she couldn't make out much of the person in the darkness, she could see the silhouette of something in his hands. A weapon, no doubt.

The shadow snapped his head around, searching the night, quickly locating the shed. The weapon was brought to bear and Misilina dived away from the window before it exploded into a thousand pieces.

'Into the roller! Quickly!' Already in the safety zone, she fired through the hole in the windowpane. Fortunately, their assailant had no cover and retreated. Misilina took the opportunity to dive into the roller too. A quick check over her shoulder confirmed that Jolan and Mandine were crouched in the back, so she gave it power and they sped across the field.

Shots sounded from behind them, raining on the ground. Whoever it was had a powerful long-range weapon. Misilina hoped that the assailant's vehicle wasn't too close.

The roller flew along. Thankfully, the field was treeless, although that also meant that there was no cover for them. And there was no doubt their pursuer would follow.

Then a thought struck her and she screeched to a halt.

'What are you doing?' Mandine demanded.

Misilina dived into the back seat and snatched Mandine's wrist communicator off before throwing it out the window and using her comm unit to blast it into pieces. Then she tore her unit apart, detaching the weapon function, which clipped to the back, and destroying the rest of it.

'Are you crazy?' Mandine screamed. 'How can anyone contact us now?'

Misilina ignored her, restarting the roller and taking off again. She heard nothing at first, but eventually, Jolan's voice broke through her distraction. 'Missy, what was that all about? Missy? What's going on?'

'Emergency protocols,' she answered, trying to watch where she was going while working out what she was going to do next.

'What?'

'Emergency protocols will be in force,' she explained. 'Even without the homing tracker, our comm devices can be traced.'

'Not on Darsair,' he said. 'I told you, their distance is severely limited here. Close range only.'

'Exactly. And whoever's following us is at close range. They followed the homing device. We can't give them anything else that will let them know where we are.'

'But no one else will know either, you idiot!' said Mandine.

'Yes, and maybe they're still on their way, but that person got there first. They're closer than anyone coming to help us. It's too dangerous to give them direct access to our locations.'

72

Yes, it was too dangerous. And irregular. And disturbing.

'Someone found us,' Misilina said. She knew she probably shouldn't be saying this aloud. 'Someone alone. Someone armed. The only reason that would happen would be if that person was there to kill us. Even if there had been an uprising and they wanted to kill us as some kind of display of power, they would have come with more than one.'

'What are you saying?' Jolan asked.

'I don't think this was anything to do with any uprising. It can't be. They wouldn't risk sending only one person to capture or kill you. A single person means only one thing.'

'That it was the sniper?'

'I think that's likely. And that means whoever it is wants to kill you, my Lord, specifically. I don't know why, but there's no doubt in my mind that's what we're dealing with here.'

Mandine's voice was fierce. 'So what are we going to do then?'

'The first thing we're going to do is find more sugar. I only have one canister left. After that, we're going to try and make our way back to the Star Runner and get out of here.' Agency protocols dictated that Tenya and the others, if they couldn't find their charges, were likely to rendezvous either there or Tekkon headquarters to make further plans. Misilina expected they would be monitoring both locations and she felt it was more sensible to head straight for a Verindonian ship. The sooner they flew out of there, the better.

'And where are you going to find sugar in the middle of nowhere?' She could almost hear Mandine's scowl.

'Every agent knows where they can find sugar in every place they visit. We need to know. It's just a question of getting there.' And that was the hard part. It didn't matter that she knew of several different locations. She had to find a way to get in and out without ending their lives.

CHAPTER EIGHT

Sarah hurried through the walkway linking the Agency's headquarters to the palace, remembering all too well the first time she'd passed that way. She had been going to save Keridan when the Agency thought he had disrespected her during his mission to retrieve her from Earth.

There was every bit as much urgency in her pace now, even though her husband—her bond-partner—was already debriefing Overlord Ardon in the throne room. This time it was their daughter who was in danger. And Ardon and Talma's youngest child.

She pushed her way through the crowds of agents and staff who hurried back and forth, all aware that a crisis had taken place, all doing what they could to help.

As she marched up to the throne room with its lukis stone-encrusted doors, she paid little attention to the swirling colours they presented. She'd seen them often enough before, especially during her time as overlord. And it definitely wasn't enough to hold her interest just then.

The guards at the door swung it open for her and she raced inside. Ardon and Talma were both on their thrones. Talma's face was still tear-stained, her blue eyes fraught; she'd been crying since they'd heard what had happened. Ardon tapped his fingers on the gilded arms on his throne, his hands running through his short brown hair. That was enough to tell her how hard he was taking the news. Talma had threatened to shave his head once if he kept running his hands through it—a habit he'd developed as the responsibilities of being overlord had started to pierce his devil-may-care facade. He hadn't done it for years ... until now.

Keridan turned as she walked in, his eyes meeting hers, his hand reaching out. She took it and stood beside him. 'Are there any updates?'

High Commander Zaden stood before the royal couple, his face set in hard lines. 'Nothing new. It's difficult to get any information out of Tekkon since the uprising started. We have several Star Runners and troop carriers ready to go but Darsair won't give us permission to even enter orbit around their planet.'

'Why would they deny us?' Talma demanded, twisting her hands together. 'They know what's at stake. We sent Jolan as a show of unity and assistance. He's fourth in the line of succession. They have to realise how imperative it is that we get word of him.'

'What do we know?' Sarah asked.

'Only what we've heard previously,' Keridan said. 'That the miners have staged an uprising and have stormed the government headquarters at Tekkon. We know that Jolan was targeted but have received no confirmation that he was killed.'

'But none that he's alive either,' Talma said bleakly.

'And his entire squad is dead?' That was the hardest part for Sarah. Nessan had graduated with Misilina and they knew his family well. They had also known Benton for some time. He had been considered for several Agency positions. And if Jolan's squad was dead, what did it mean for Mandine's? What did it mean for Jolan himself?

Ardon rubbed his forehead. 'Do you want me to order the Darsair government to let us land? Even if they can't clear us somewhere in Tekkon, surely we can take advantage at a nearby port, say in Grasslen or Dormer? Once we're on the ground, we can get in.'

Zaden nodded. 'We're trying to gain permission, my Lord, but the Darsairian government is reluctant to give it. It's clear they're worried about how it will look if we have to stop this uprising for them.'

'Surely they can see past that!' Talma's voice squeaked high with nerves.

'I understand that, my Lady,' said Zaden, 'but they don't care.

I was as forceful as I could be, making it clear it was unacceptable to have one of our overlord's children vulnerable on their planet and practically ordering them to let us land, but they started making noises about considering it an invasion. You know how that would look to the Government of the Seven Systems. They've been working hard at cleaning up things on Darsair for years. It's only been with their help that the planet's gained its new respectability. Having us land a force anywhere without their approval could be taken as an act of war.'

'So there's nothing we can do?' Sarah's eyes explored Keridan's face. Surely he, the master of strategy, could find a way?

His scowl was all the answer she needed. 'We need to stay on good terms with them or we'll get no information at all. But keep up the pressure, Zaden, or I can, if you like. We have to get them to let us land.'

It had been a long time since Ardon had looked so serious. Things had been peaceful on Verindon for years, apart from a minor crisis here or there, and Sarah was accustomed to his relaxed style of leadership, so different from her own. But his expression was as bleak as Talma's. 'I knew we shouldn't have sent them with so little protection but Utreysin ensured us there would be no problems. I should have listened to my instincts.'

'Try not to dwell on it, my Lord,' said Keridan. 'We'll get them out.'

The door opened again, Sarah turning with a frown. They were supposed to be left alone.

'Councillor Veston, my Lord,' announced one of the guards.

That explained it. Mandine's father, come to find out the latest himself.

Sarah hadn't met Veston before his daughter had become engaged to Jolan; his family had never been prominent in elite circles. Having met him twice, she'd thought that was enough, but she felt every sympathy for him as he hurried into the room, his face pinched with worry, his eyes determined.

'My Lord.' He bowed, his eyes passing over everyone in the room. 'Forgive this intrusion but I must find out the latest from

Darsair. Is there any word?'

'*He's fat, entitled and a trifle too ambitious for me to take him seriously,*' Ardon had told her when he'd revealed they would soon welcome a daughter-in-law into their family. But now he was everything patient; this was Ardon at his best. 'I'm sorry, no, councillor. We're keeping every channel of communication open and I assure you, the moment we hear anything we will inform you immediately.'

The councillor's expression dissolved into anger. 'The Darsairians are still shutting us out? Surely they must recognise the disgrace they would be under if we lost any member of the royal family on their soil.'

'They want to try and sort things out themselves first,' said Zaden. 'We've made allowances for that, but there will come a point when we press the issue.'

'We must press it now,' Veston insisted. 'I need my daughter home.' He turned back to Ardon. 'She, as you well know, my Lord, is my only kin. How can I rest until she's back by my side?'

Talma rose from her throne, stepped down from the dais, and took his hands. It was so typical of her to do something like that, but also against protocol. Sarah could tell the councillor knew the honour he was receiving as his chest puffed out.

'I understand how you feel,' she said, tears gathering on her lids. 'I feel the same fear for my boy. My youngest son.' She blinked back her sorrow and smiled at Keridan and Sarah. 'I know my friends here also feel it with their daughter in danger as well. But we must believe that they will all come home safe and unharmed. And I have no doubt they will.'

Lie. The word sounded in Sarah's head. She knew Talma *wanted* to believe it, but she was far from certain.

Veston's response held the same element of doubt. 'I'm sure you're right, my Lady.' Then he turned to Zaden and Keridan. 'But surely we can send more experienced agents to Darsair? Indeed, why didn't more experienced agents go with them in the first place?'

Keridan's eyes flashed. 'Agents Benton and Tenya are both highly experienced and, given the progress Darsair had made recently in keeping the peace on their planet, it was deemed suitable that some high-performing graduates should be included in the party. Although we knew there were small pockets of unrest there, they weren't represented as the danger they have turned out to be.'

The councillor pursed his lips. 'Maybe next time you'll take more care.'

Keridan shot a warning glance in Sarah's direction as she stepped forward. How dare he? Ardon didn't look impressed either. 'I had no problem with their selection of agents, and given that my son was the primary recipient of their care, I think that if anyone should be banging their fist in outrage, it's me.'

Talma stepped towards him, but he sat back in his throne with a sigh as the councillor looked contrite. 'My apologies, my Lord. I didn't mean to accuse you of anything.'

Talma gave him a reassuring smile. 'Of course you didn't.'

'Councillor, we *will* get all the party back,' said Zaden, Sarah's lie detector again tinkling in the back of her head. 'Please, return to your chambers and we'll contact you as soon as there's news.'

Talma took his hands and even went so far as to lead him to the door. 'Don't worry, Councillor Veston, your daughter will be safe.'

The councillor gave a watery smile. 'I'm sure she will, my Lady.' Then, taking both her hands in his, he bowed over them. 'Thank you for your concern.'

After the door had shut behind him, Ardon rolled his eyes and addressed the guards on the doors. 'Under no account is he to be admitted again unless we give express permission.'

Talma frowned at him. 'Ardon, be kind. He's worried about his daughter.'

'No, he isn't.' The words forced their way out of Sarah's mouth.

Keridan had been watching her intently and instantly came to her side. 'What's wrong?'

Sarah felt dizzy as her mind tried to work out what it meant. 'He wasn't lying.'

'Councillor Veston?'

'Yes.' Sarah turned to Talma, the only other lie detector in the room. 'Did you get anything?'

She looked puzzled. 'I'm sorry, Sarah. The only lie I picked up from him was when he agreed with me that they would all be safe.'

'Yes, I know. That was the only time he lied. But it wasn't the only time you lied. You lied when you told him you were sure his daughter would be safe. And he agreed with you. But he *wasn't* lying.'

Talma looked befuddled. 'So?'

'He lied when he agreed that everyone would be safe but was *telling the truth* when he agreed that his daughter would be safe.'

Keridan's face paled. 'So why he is sure about one but not the other?'

Sarah could tell when Ardon and Zaden realised. Talma still looked clueless and Ardon explained as Zaden approached his two fellow agents. 'What do you think it means?'

'I'm not sure exactly what, but I know one thing,' said Keridan, his face grim. 'I want to take a closer look at Councillor Veston. *Everything* about the councillor.'

Zaden nodded. 'I'll tell Pravvit you're coming to see him.'

CHAPTER NINE

Misilina knew that the trickiest thing about finding sugar in Tekkon wouldn't be locating it; she knew six different locations she could try. No, the hardest part was picking the right target because their enemy—whoever it was—must have realised she needed it too and would be waiting for them there.

Should she try and reach Tekkon's government headquarters first? She'd considered that, but couldn't dismiss the possibility that this attack was their idea. Also, she hadn't even seen any crowd control forces during their journey through the city. She imagined they were busy trying to quell unrest in the streets. Either that or they were deliberately avoiding them in the hope the miners would find them first and destroy them.

No, she wouldn't feel safe unless she was contacted by a Verindonian. And even if that did happen, which was hard now they had no communicators, she needed to have access to more sugar, just in case she had to fight off either crowds or crowd control. She hoped it wouldn't come to that. While she was sure she'd put up a good fight, if an angry mob came at them, she wouldn't have the skills to fight them off *and* keep them from killing Jolan.

She considered going directly to the Star Runner and flying Jolan and Mandine home herself. She'd received an above-average result in her piloting modules, but piloting that model of Star Runner single-handedly would be tricky. It was likely that Jolan would be able to help her, though, and she knew the ship could fly acceptably with two.

But even then, she would likely need more sugar in case they ran into trouble trying to get into the landing bay.

So if she was assessing protocols correctly, sugar was the highest priority. It would be dangerous to go to the first or last choices on her list. They would be too obvious. She needed to decide between locations two, three, four or five and hope that the enemy didn't pick the right one. She didn't tell this to either Jolan or Mandine. There was no need to worry them. She wished she could go by herself but that was impossible. She couldn't leave them unguarded.

Eventually, she decided on location four. It was a factory about a third of the way into the city itself. Their stores of sugar weren't huge, but they had sufficient quantities of canned sugar. That was the easiest to carry on her. She, Jolan and Mandine could all keep some cans on them. That should give her enough to get them out of there. They could handle four, maybe five cans each, although Mandine's outfit didn't seem to be fitted with pockets. They could store some in the vehicle as well, but she knew they might have to abandon it, so she couldn't rely on anything they left there.

Jolan remained silent as she started back for Tekkon but Mandine did not. 'It's about time,' she sniffed. 'We should have gone back ages ago.'

'We tried that,' said Jolan.

'Yes, but the rebels are hardly going to be blocking every route, are they? And even if they are, crowd control is bound to be there. We should be looking for them.'

Misilina didn't want to explain why she thought that was a bad idea. She also couldn't be bothered reminding her that they had limited places to enter on their side of the city. Every road that led in was too close to miners' homes to be considered safe. Even as she turned down road after road, trying to find some way in, she still frequently had to retreat as rioters came into view. It took almost a maxispan before she even managed to get a street length within the city's boundary.

Once there, she kept her eyes on everything, including the

passengers in the back seat, making sure they kept their heads down. Every so often, Jolan lifted his for a peek.

'My Lord,' she said for the fifth time, 'please keep your head down. It's too dangerous.'

But he ignored her, sitting up further. 'You need extra eyes and ears. You won't get through if you have to do it all yourself.'

She wanted to snap at him, but he quickly proved his usefulness, pointing to an alleyway she'd forgotten about. 'Down there.'

The roller barely fit, scraping the sides as she drove slowly through. Once they reached the end of the alley, she crawled out through the roller's broken roof so she could peer around the corner.

Jolan came to join her. 'Which way are we headed?'

She nodded to the left. 'Down here. Still a few streets away, though.' She drew him back from the corner as they heard voices and the sound of windows breaking.

Jolan grimaced. 'The looters are having fun.'

'That's not our concern,' said Misilina. 'Keeping you safe is all that matters.'

'But we're getting sugar first, not getting out of here?'

'If I don't have sugar, I can't defend you. I'm going to need more than one can.' She still hadn't lost hope that Tenya and the others were looking for them. Not having a comm unit made contacting them difficult but she was a resourceful agent. Surely she could find a way.

He licked his lips. 'I hope we can make it.'

Mandine's wheedling voice rang out. 'Are you two going to stand there all day or are we going to move?'

Jolan's patience was wearing thin; Misilina could see it in his eyes. 'We're just waiting until everything is clear,' he said.

'That's all we ever do,' Mandine grumbled.

Jolan gave Misilina a look that was half-apology and half-frustration. 'Don't give me that look,' she said. 'You're the one who's bonding with her.' The moment the words were out, she regretted them.

He was not her childhood friend anymore. It was an eon since they'd been friends. He was now one of her leaders and also the man she was trying to protect. She had no business speaking to him like that.

She opened her mouth to apologise but his eyes snapped with fire. 'Well, maybe you don't know everything. Maybe if you actually paid attention to the world beyond proving you're a living, breathing asset to the Agency, you might understand.'

His tone made her seethe. Her rule-keeping side pleaded with her to make peace, to show him the respect his station deserved, but a million different memories of Jolan the needler, Jolan the brat, Jolan her tormentor—setting her hair on fire, teasing her mercilessly, playing countless pranks—passed through her mind. 'I do understand. I understand that you like brainless women on your arm. Maybe they make you feel smart.' She had definitely thrown caution to the wind.

She expected another stinging retort. She didn't expect him to pull up in shock. The look he gave her seemed almost contrite. 'She's not that bad.'

'The words of an awestruck lover if ever I heard them.'

His reply was bitter. 'Since when have elite bondings been about love?'

'Since *your* parents bonded, since *my* parents bonded ...'

'They're the exception, and you know that. Cress has still been given a list of twenty women that he's to use to choose a bond-partner. Tesrin's list is a little longer, given that he's second-in-line. Tilla will get one soon too. Hers will probably be the same length as mine; longer than either of my brothers.' He looked over his shoulder, checking that Mandine wasn't listening, Misilina thought.

It looked like she was polishing her nails. 'And Mandine barely even made it onto your list,' she said. 'Her family aren't exactly prominent.' She gave a smug smile at his surprised expression. 'Yes, I do pay attention. I know all about your list.'

His mouth twisted. 'I'm sure it made interesting reading for you.'

She tossed her head. 'Only from an objective standpoint. I was mildly curious as to why you picked the last name on it.'

She expected another biting reply, but the fire left his eyes. He looked around again. 'Did you know she started five charities on her own? And two of them she created anonymously. She didn't want the glory; she just wanted to do good. One of them was Make Mines Safe.'

'I thought that was your mother's charity.'

'Mandine gave it to her. She didn't want to be the frontrunner of that one. She thought Mother would do it better. She just wanted to get the work done and she was stretched so thin with her other charities that she didn't have the time for it.' He gave her a pleading look. 'I know she's shallow and that she thinks too much about her looks and her clothes, but so does *every* girl on my list. And my brothers'. But at least she believes in something. She believes in helping people. She reminds me of Mother when she talks about her work. She really does care for people. She just doesn't always know how to show it.'

Misilina cast her eyes over Mandine again. Could she have misjudged her? She could make the excuse that she'd only had access to limited information, but even now she found it difficult to believe in her, difficult to *like* her. She could feel her resentment resisting the change. She didn't want to like Mandine and there was no rational reason for that. She was her assignment. She shouldn't feel like this.

She looked back at Jolan. The look on his face, the eyes pleading for understanding, brought to mind the good times—the games they'd played together, the fun they'd had. The time when he'd found the tunnels underneath the palace and they'd hidden down there for maxispans while everyone searched for them, giggling and exploring. The times when he'd helped her reach the highest shelves because he'd been so much taller than her.

Yes, there had been good times that she'd buried beneath bad memories. Before he'd become Lord Jolan, instead of just Jolan, her buddy. Before he'd started to hang out with only the Verindal elite and looked down his nose at her. Before he'd failed to defend her when she'd been teased for being a crossbreed. That was when she'd started to magnify those moments he'd needled her, teased her, annoyed her, giving them precedence over everything in her mind.

But regardless of their childhood, regardless of any of these memories or what they meant, it didn't change the fact that he was now a lord of their planet about to be bonded to a brainless fool, and that both of them were in her charge and she needed to keep them safe and get them home.

CHAPTER TEN

Sarah and Keridan headed straight for Pravvit's apartment. His bond-partner, Perisina, met them at the door. She was unflustered, as usual, the touch of grey in her jet-black hair glinting in the light. It made Perisina look distinguished, Sarah realised in passing, whereas she still used a virtual program to hide her greys.

Perisina smiled but got straight down to business. 'Zaden contacted us and Pravvit's already begun his search.'

They were ushered into the relatively small apartment. Pravvit and Perisina's three children had their own apartments now and it hadn't taken long for their father to reclaim the space. In place of comm devices and virtual training aids were numerous virtual screens with workpanels in front of them, all running long lengths of data and figures that were gobbledygook to Sarah but would be as plain as day to Pravvit.

Pravvit had his eyeglasses on, the circles on his irises flashing as he looked away from the screen and the setting on them adjusted so he could see his friends clearly. Years of staring at screens had taken their toll on his dark eyes, and his back had a slight but permanent bend to it. His hair had a few more threads of grey than his bond-partner, but he never seemed to care.

'I wondered when I'd see you,' he said. 'I've been running various scenarios since Zaden told me what happened.' He pointed out some virtual simulations on the monitors. He had recreated the events from the riot and Sarah could see it play out in several different ways. She turned away as she saw her daughter fall to the ground, dead. That was one outcome she hoped was wrong.

'Did he tell you the latest?' Keridan asked.

'You want me to look into Councillor Veston. I've been dissecting everything I can find.' He waved them over and they looked at the screen before them. 'I've isolated a couple of things I'm concerned about.'

A wealth of data assailed Sarah's eyes and she waited, mostly patiently, for Pravvit to explain it to them.

'I've hacked into his message systems, both his private and business accounts.'

Keridan nodded. 'Yes, he's been involved in mining for most of his life.'

'Grate mining, low-grade gem mining. His isalite mines have been showing a drop in revenue for some time, apparently.'

Isalite was a cheaper version of lukis. 'Yes, Selli and Lina have been complaining about the quality of isalite gems lately,' said Perisina. 'Lina wanted some for her coming-of-age celebrations but there was little to be found.'

Sarah remembered that from when they'd attended the celebrations. Both of Pravvit and Perisina's girls had graduated from the Academy within a year of each other and had had their coming-of-age celebrations exactly a year apart. Selli had given Lina an isalite bracelet, apologising all the while that it wasn't as stunning as she'd hoped. But Lina took after her mother so had replied with a calm smile and sisterly reassurance.

'And grate rock isn't in demand,' Keridan said. 'I don't know why it's still being mined.'

'Yes,' Pravvit confirmed. 'However, we know he tried to buy a lukis mine from Councillor Frodam recently.'

Sarah frowned. 'If his other mines are doing that badly it's a wonder he had funds for that.'

Pravvit made a non-committal noise. 'He received some of his bond-partner's estates when she passed on to the next life a few years ago, but her resources weren't vast either. Hmm.' He stopped talking and peered at the screen.

'What?' asked Keridan, looking over his shoulder.

'He's recently had some deposits to his credit line. Sizeable ones, too.'

A tight feeling hit Sarah in the chest. 'Any idea where from?'

'Give me a moment.' Pravvit sent information flying, his eyeline bringing other things to the fore as he focused on files and data. It was all too much of a jumble for Sarah to follow.

'Huh,' he said finally. 'It's well-hidden. I wonder why?'

'How long will it take you to find out?' Keridan asked.

Pravvit held out his hand. 'Fancy a wager?'

That brought a scowl from Sarah. 'Pravvit, my daughter's life is in danger, and Ardon and Talma's boy, who's in the line of succession. Are you really going to waste time be—'

He smirked. 'Got it.'

Keridan glanced at her, raising his eyebrows apologetically. Perisina smiled the usual smile she wore when Pravvit was up to something. Sarah tried to calm herself so she could absorb whatever information he had.

Then he blanched. 'Keridan, the Icho Company is on Darsair, isn't it?'

Sarah felt the colour flee from her face as Keridan looked closer at what the search had revealed. Pravvit nodded soberly. 'Those deposits were from the Icho Company.'

'The main mining business in Tekkon,' Keridan said. 'A lot of the members of Tekkon's government have stakes in that company. Are you sure? It would seem stupid for them to implicate themselves via an illegal payment. Someone isn't trying to frame them?'

Pravvit crossed his arms. 'Keridan, please give me some credit. Do you really think that just because I found it that it was easy to find?'

Sarah nodded. Pravvit found connections no matter how deeply they were buried.

'The strikes and allegations of safety issues hit them hard.' She could see Keridan's brain working a mile a minute as he spoke. 'There's only one reason they would be paying him.'

Sarah closed her eyes, hoping to block out the truth. 'Please tell me it was for some mining equipment.'

'Sorry, Sarah,' Pravvit said. 'It's in his private account, and well-hidden. This was, as they say on Earth, an under-the-table deal. It's something he didn't intend for anyone to find.'

'So some kind of bribe or agreement.' Keridan stroked his chin. 'See what else you can find out.'

But although Pravvit searched for a maxispan, he couldn't find any details on what it was for. 'The councillor has visited Darsair on business trips. He could well have made this deal while he was there.'

Keridan nodded. 'We need to find out what it was about.'

'How do you propose we do that?' asked Perisina. 'The Mind Warden?'

Sarah shuddered. Although officially called an interrogation device, the Mind Warden could be used to torture people. Keridan had endured it after they'd returned from Earth, and it had killed the woman she'd known as her mother.

'No, regardless of these payments, I don't think we could justify an action as extreme as that. It would be much easier to catch him in a lie.' He looked at Sarah.

She was ready for anything, especially if it saved Misilina. 'What do you want me to do?'

***

Sarah had never been one for games of hide and seek, not that this could be called a game. But as Keridan drew back the drapery behind Ardon's throne and she crawled inside, it seemed more than a little bizarre.

As she settled into her hidey-hole and Keridan pulled the drapes around her, hiding her completely, Ardon coughed. 'Testing, one two, one two.'

She rolled her eyes. 'I can hear you just fine, Ardon, since I'm sitting right behind you.'

He drew back the curtain and stuck his head in. 'That's "my Lord" to you.'

'Ugh!' Even with his son's life in danger, he could still play the fool.

Keridan readjusted the drapes and she settled back in as her bond-partner lowered his voice. 'Sarah, can you still hear me?'

'Yes.'

'Good. Councillor Veston isn't a soft speaker, but you need to be able to hear everything he says. That way you'll get a clearer read on him. It will be just him and Ardon and a few male guards, so he won't be worrying about any lie detectors. Hopefully, that will make him speak freely.'

'You aren't staying?' she asked.

'No, he might not be as unguarded if I'm here. Just listen carefully to everything he says and see what you can find out.'

She huddled back down into her hidey-hole, trying to ignore the urge to sneeze. She stifled it, listening carefully. It was a few moments before she heard the dull sound of the door opening.

'Councillor Veston, my Lord,' said one of the door guards.

She heard the thud of Ardon's footsteps as he trod down from the dais to greet him. She hoped he wasn't going to do something out of character like embrace him. Even the loss of his son's life wouldn't make Ardon act like that.

'My Lord, how is the situation?' The councillor's voice sounded rushed. 'I came as soon as I got your message. Is there news from Darsair?'

Keridan had given Ardon strict instructions on what he should say, with the hope that he would be convincing. 'I'm sorry, councillor,' he said, his voice throbbing with uncustomary sincerity.

'For what, my Lord?' peeped Veston. He sounded surprised.

'We have received word from our people on Darsair. I'm sorry to tell you that it has been confirmed that there was an uprising, led by a group of rebel miners. Your daughter lost her life, along with those of all her agent guards.'

Sarah felt her own heart thud heavily. This was the story they'd fabricated, but it could be true, for all they knew. And if it was, her daughter was dead.

There was no sound from Veston for some time. When he finally spoke, his voice was low and confused. 'I don't understand.'

'Your daughter has been killed. I'm sorry. Her body is being returned to Verindon as we speak.'

There was another stretch of silence. 'And your son?'

'His life was spared, fortunately. He is returning with a contingent of agents.'

The councillor made a strange noise. A sob? No, he still seemed confused more than anything. 'Are you sure?' was the next response.

'Yes, it has been confirmed.'

'I don't ... I can't ...'

Then the faint sound of sobbing could be heard, followed by Ardon's soft voice again. 'I'm so sorry. I know how devastating this news must be.'

His voice was so caring and genuine. Who knew he could be such a good actor?

But now for the crucial part of the conversation. 'There is something, though, that has puzzled us about this.'

She could hear the grief in Veston's voice as he replied, 'Yes, my Lord?' But it was more than grief. It was shock as well, she thought, but not the shock she might have expected. She homed in on every word.

'Apparently, your daughter left the care of her guard. They pursued her, unsure of where she was, and eventually located her, but not in time to save her or themselves. She was located in a secret base that had been used by the rebels to plot their action. Do you have any idea why she would have been there?'

'None, my Lord.'

Lie. The word clamoured in Sarah's head.

'We're also trying to fathom how she even knew about it, especially since Tekkon's government didn't. Any insights?'

'I can't imagine, my Lord.'

Lie.

'We have been wondering the same thing. It's like she knew where they were and went there purposefully.'

The councillor tried to put some indignation into his voice. It was so manufactured she was sure Ardon would pick it up without her assistance. 'She would never do such a thing, my Lord!'

Lie, lie, lie.

There was such a long silence Sarah imagined she could hear the dust swirling throughout the room. Then Ardon spoke again. 'Are you *really* sure, councillor?'

He's definitely picked up on it. And even if he hadn't, Sarah had heard enough. She drew back the drapes and stepped out, the councillor's face paling at the sight of her. 'Really, *really* sure?' she said.

Councillor Veston bleated as Keridan came through the door, a contingent of guards with him. 'Councillor Veston, you're under arrest on suspicion of treason and conspiracy to endanger the life of a member of the High Family of Verindon.'

'B-but I didn't!'

At least now Sarah could verbalise it. 'Lie.'

'But my Lord,' whined the councillor, 'please, it wasn't my doing. It wasn't even my idea. I didn't want to betray you. My hand was forced!'

Ardon strolled back to his throne with a sigh. 'Take him away and get a full confession. I don't want all the details, just the basics, like if *my son is still alive!*'

As they dragged the still pleading councillor away, Keridan took Sarah's hands. 'He was lying?'

But now there was doubt. 'Mostly.'

Keridan's eyebrows furrowed. 'Mostly?'

'You could have fooled me,' snorted Ardon.

'It's true he was lying about not knowing why Mandine might have been somewhere unexpected. But he was telling the truth when he said it wasn't his idea, that he hadn't wanted to do it. Whoever masterminded this, it wasn't him.'

Keridan pondered that. 'I'd better go back and see Pravvit then in case he's dug anything else up.' He turned to Ardon. 'Or would you prefer that I supervise the councillor's interrogation?'

'By all means, Keridan, go and deal with the councillor. Pravvit will be only too glad to tell us any new developments. He's more fond of scandal than a miner's bond-partner. And I think your glower in Veston's face will loosen his tongue faster than anything else we've got, even the Mind Warden.'

Keridan bowed. 'Certainly.' And with a smile at Sarah, he left the room.

'It's puzzling, that's for sure,' Ardon said.

'Hmm.' Sarah wasn't sure how else to respond. Her mind was still dissecting the councillor's responses. Then she woke up to her responsibilities. 'I'll go check in with Pravvit, my Lord.'

'Certainly. Let me know what he says.'

Before she could turn for the door, Ardon spoke again. 'And Sarah?'

'Yes, my Lord?'

His eyes bore a sincerity she rarely saw there. 'I *will* see our children returned to us.'

His words reminded her of a time, so long ago, when she and Ardon were to have been bonded. It seemed so far from reality now it was difficult to believe it had ever happened. They had found better partners—people who complemented them. So it was for the best that that future had not come to pass.

But that hadn't changed their bond. Not the bond of lovers, but one of sturdy respect. And even though she knew his words were just wishful thinking, a desperate plea for a conclusion that wouldn't devastate them both, she believed it anyway.

'Thank you, my Lord.'

CHAPTER ELEVEN

Misilina finally found a road that was both quiet and direct enough to get them to the factory. It was in a part of the city she never would have dreamt of taking members of the high family, but she had little choice.

The building had a power-wire fence—the wire of the barrier made of energy. The factory itself was square, ugly and dark. She could see stains on the walls—long dripping marks left by smoke belching from the stacks on its roof. She could smell the stale air of baking and her stomach turned. It smelled nothing like the things they baked on Verindon.

At least she knew exactly where she needed to go—she'd studied the blueprints and communications of all sugar stores before she'd left home. Enyi had thought it was overkill, but it would benefit them now.

Her heart constricted at the thought of Enyi, but she couldn't let it distract her.

After sitting out the front for a few minspans, making sure there was no sound or movement from within, she turned to Jolan and Mandine. 'We're going to have to go in. You'll both need to come with me, as this isn't a safe area. Even without the rebel miners, I can't risk leaving you here.'

'Sure,' said Jolan with a nod. Mandine rolled her eyes.

'I'll create a door in the fence so we can get through. I'll lead the way; I know exactly where their sugar stores are. We'll get what we can carry and get out as quickly as possible.' It sounded easy, but it would be far from that if their enemy was there. She still hoped that the enemy was one person alone. If so, there was a one in six chance they would find her.

But what if there's a group of them? What if they can station people at each place?

She couldn't think like that. There was no other way.

Mandine folded her arms. 'Why should I go in there?'

If there was one thing Misilina hated it was stating the obvious, especially if she'd already done it once. She tried to keep her voice neutral. By the look on Jolan's face, she failed. 'Because I need to make sure both of you are safe and you won't be out here.'

'Ugh!' Mandine said and burst into tears.

That made Jolan's gaze soften and he took her in his arms. 'It's all right, sweetheart. I know this is terrible, but if we can get Missy some sugar, it increases our chance of getting home safely. That's all I want. Okay?'

She raised her eyes to his, tears on her lids, one dropping over and tracking a silvery trail down her face. 'Yes, that's all I want too. I want us to be home and safe. Together forever.' She smiled through her tears.

Misilina felt her back stiffen. She grabbed at the front seat of the roller, her fingers digging into its surface, as she tried to work out what had just happened. For as Mandine had spoken, one word had clanged inside her head.

Lie.

She had to be imagining things. She was probably projecting her dislike of Mandine into her thought patterns. There was no way she could have really detected a lie. She had never done that before. It was the joke David always played on her, lying to see if she could pick it up. She never did when he tried it. Why would she suddenly start now?

She saw Jolan glance at her as the word continued to flash on and off in her thoughts, like an alert in a lukis mine. She shook her head to clear it. She had to stop being ridiculous and keep her mind on the job. These kinds of petty distractions saw missions fail and agents die.

But still, the word persisted, her head pulsing with it.

She ignored it and got out of the roller, the other two following.

Then it was up to the fence. With nothing but the weapon function left on her comm unit, she broke into the switch box near the wall, grateful it wasn't a high-security location. There was a low squeal as she programmed it for door function. A section of the fence vanished and she ducked though. 'Quickly.'

They hurried through the gap. Misilina hoped no one would come by and see it. She couldn't risk shutting it in case they needed to make a hasty exit.

With whisper-soft footfalls, Misilina approached the building, trying to ignore the sound of Jolan's step and Mandine's all-too-obvious shuffle. She motioned for both of them to stick close to the building, standing in the shadows out of the one feeble light that shone on the factory's loading bay.

The interior was dark and stank of leftover food, even though they'd stepped into a dingy office. She wrinkled her nose, but continued through to the other side of the room where there was a door that linked to the factory floor. That was where she wanted to be. She wished she still had the light function on her comm unit to help avoid the desk and ancient chairs positioned around.

The door on the other side was as primitive as the furniture. It had hinges and even a grip to twist before it opened! She'd only seen things like that in vids. She slipped through, the others behind her. Then it was down a short corridor. The door at the end wasn't locked either, but its hinges creaked, the sound breaking the silence.

They entered a cavernous room with machinery from floor to ceiling. Large vats were linked to each other via a network of pipes, terminating in a few conveyor belts. She could hear the soft hum of some machinery—a cold room by the sound of it—its purr like a sentinel guarding the factory from the dark.

But the dark was where Misilina was going. That wonderful purr from the cold room. That was their destination—where their sugar canisters were stored.

A feeble light hanging above cut a path through the dark as they picked their way across the factory floor.

It was a whisper, so soft she would have missed it if it hadn't happened between their steps, a click that she would never have heard otherwise. She dived on Jolan, using the force of her fall to push him behind a curl of machinery pipe. 'Get down!' she screamed at Mandine.

But the woman just stood there, hands on hips. 'You save *him*. *I'm* your assignment and you choose to save *him*!'

She was about to drag her to safety, but to Misilina's amazement, Keily stepped out of the shadows. Mandine's lady-in-waiting was no longer dressed serviceably, holding out a gown for her mistress. She was in a black jumpsuit and had a laser rifle slung across her shoulders.

Mandine turned and walked away. 'Hurry up and shoot them.'

But Misilina had gone into the safety zone when she'd tackled Jolan and her weapon was aimed before the words had passed Mandine's lips. Keily dived for cover.

Misilina barely noticed the shock on Jolan's face. It was a relief he didn't appeal to Mandine or ask any stupid questions. It was not the time. Fortunately, their cover was the start of a long stretch of piping. She pushed Jolan along before spraying Keily's hiding place with fire. The pipe continued to curl around and they followed it, Misilina shooting behind her, hoping to keep the girl pinned down.

Misilina fingered the final can of sugar that was slung at her belt. She could smell the stores of it in the factory, so tantalisingly close to them, but she couldn't risk going for it now. Keily would be expecting that.

But soon she would have to come out of the safety zone and one more transformation was all that stood between them and death.

She continued to hustle Jolan along, hearing Mandine's impatient voice behind them. 'You haven't got them yet? I thought you were supposed to be the best. Destroy the sugar stores. That's what she wants.'

'We need to get over there,' Misilina told Jolan. She pointed to a conveyor belt. Behind it was the door to a side office. 'Go. I'll cover you.' She sprayed fire everywhere as Jolan made his move, following him, putting herself between him and where she felt Keily was most likely to be.

She sensed the shots coming from above and kept moving. Keily shifted to the side and Misilina met her shots as well.

She jumped up to open the office door and she and Jolan raced inside. Fortunately, the door was another old-fashioned one. 'Quick,' she said, grabbing the furniture nearby. Jolan helped her push it up against the door. Soon she could hear Keily trying to break in. She didn't seem to be trying too hard, though, and that was what Misilina had hoped for. It meant that while her assailant had studied the blueprints for this place, she wasn't as thorough as Misilina. Keily thought they were trapped in this boxy little room.

But there had been a recent renovation—an air vent inserted into the outer wall of the office. There had been a long stream of internal messages about having it put in. No one else usually thought to read that far.

She took hold of the grill over the vent and removed the cooling system in front of it, precious microspans wasted as she had to force the latches since she had no comm unit program to release them. Trying to ignore the sounds of Keily's determined efforts to reach them and Jolan piling up everything he could to put in her way, Misilina removed the cooling system, the vent, then motioned to Jolan to follow her.

There was no one outside, thankfully. As soon as Jolan was through, she raced for the power fence. Fortunately, Keily hadn't slipped outside to close the entrance she'd made. Either she hadn't had time or had assumed she would have no trouble killing them. They both dived through.

'The roller,' said Jolan.

'We can't take it.'

'Why not?'

'Because she knows about it. It's too dangerous now.' Hopefully, it wouldn't be long before they found something else.

But the worst thing that happened was the feeling of the safety zone fading away. She quickly downed her final can of sugar. That was it. She could go into the safety zone once more, and after that, she would be defenceless. She knew she would need every advantage in order to keep Jolan safe.

And there was something else she had to do. She smashed her weapon against the nearest wall.

Jolan gasped. 'What are you doing? How are you going to protect us without that?'

'She used something to track us,' said Misilina, crushing the fallen pieces into the ground under her feet. 'You don't have your wrist comm anymore. Neither does Mandine. This is the only thing she could have used.'

'What if Mandine used something else? She could have ...' his voice trailed off. She didn't think he wanted to spend too much time thinking about exactly what Mandine had done.

And he was right. Mandine could have done something to notify Keily. But it could also have been Misilina's weapon. Keily could have been tracking Verindonian tech somehow. As much as she knew they needed it, it was too great a risk.

She looked around and saw a dark alley. 'This way.' They needed to get lost in the darkness as soon as possible.

But what did she do now? They were in the middle of a rebellion. She had no sugar. She had no weapon. And there was an assassin desperate to end their lives.

There was only one thing in their favour—Misilina's memory. She knew every part of this city. Even in the dark of this alley, she knew which street was to the left and right, which were after those, how far away the government sector was and the quickest way there. Other places that had sugar. Weapon stores. It was all inside her head, a jumble of information that was no longer useless or random. It was the key to their survival.

CHAPTER TWELVE

They spent the first maxispan running and sneaking from shadow to shadow. The sound of feet or voices made Misilina freeze until they'd gone.

She considered getting off the streets. Tekkon still had sewers and they could be a useful passageway at times. She was thankful she hadn't mentioned them when Mandine had been with them, but then they'd had the roller, and they couldn't take it down there.

But she decided against the sewers, at that point, at least. The plans she'd seen of them in this section of the city looked like they hadn't been updated for decades, so how reliable were they? And there weren't a lot of entry points in this part of the city either, so it wouldn't mean less time spent on the streets.

Jolan said nothing as they crept along. He didn't nod or respond to any instruction she gave. He just followed her lead, his face a calm mask. But he had to be hurting, didn't he? Mandine, the woman he was going to bond with, had betrayed him. Tried to have him killed. Misilina was searching for reasons, trying to dissect her motives and what she might do next.

While Keily was likely the expert, Mandine might not allow her to call all the shots. Misilina couldn't imagine her listening to a woman she clearly regarded as an underling, allowing her to decide on the best course of action and commit to it. That might be what had saved them.

It was pure conjecture, of course, just like every other theory repeating in her head. Why agree to bond with a member of the high family and then try to kill him? Did she really think no one would discover what she'd done? Could she have been sure they would even pull it off? Why risk herself—she had also been in the firing line when Jolan had given his speech. It was clear he'd been the one in Keily's sights, but that didn't mean Mandine had been safe. Keily would have known, just as Misilina knew, what could go wrong in that type of operation. After all, she hadn't scored a direct hit on Jolan so far. Perhaps Mandine hadn't been concerned about the danger. Maybe her endgame had blinded her to it. Maybe she'd enjoyed the adrenaline rush.

Jolan doubled over beside her, hands on his knees, as they dived back into the darkness. 'Give me a moment.'

She was tempted to deny it, but she was exhausted too. 'Not for long.'

'What do we do now?' His head stayed down even as his breathing slowed. He wouldn't look at her. What would this do to him?

That wasn't her business. She needed to stay focused on the only thing that mattered—getting him home alive. 'Our objective hasn't changed. The first order of business is to find some more sugar for me. Without it, I can't defend you against someone like that. We need every advantage we can get.'

'But she'll know that, won't she? That's where she'll be waiting.'

'I don't believe she just happened to choose the place where we went. She was far too ready. That's why I destroyed the comm weapon. We can find other weapons, but we can't risk keeping the likely method she used to track us.'

Jolan straightened up and stepped further into the shadows. His face was still calm and blank. In shock, maybe? She catalogued what she would need to do if that was the case.

'But how can we find sugar?' His voice sounded hollow, empty, bereft. Her hand twitched towards him.

But he was no longer her childhood friend. He was now a leader and she was his security detail. Best to keep that in mind. 'It's all right, Jolan, I know where everything is. Well, most things. I had catalogued six locations that were likely to have sugar—'

'And Mandine knew them all,' he snapped.

She set her teeth, holding the glare inside. He was hurting and that was leaking through. She needed to remain professional. 'Yes, but while there are no *significant* stores anywhere else, there are many other locations where a small store is held.' Less than she probably needed, but she couldn't afford to be picky. 'Come on, we have to keep moving.'

On she led him, steering clear of rumbles of dissent or sounds of rebellion. But the smaller sounds were the bigger problems now—the soft footfalls, the creeping in the shadows, the whisper of a weapon being brought to bear. These were things she was afraid of hearing and also afraid to miss.

At least they were likely to have lost Keily. Misilina was going nowhere in particular. There was nothing to predict.

But how good was she? By her skill set, Misilina was betting she was a Jindarian. The natives of Jindar were warriors of the highest order, well-trained in every form of combat, in strategy, in survival, basically everything she'd need to carry out her assignment. Misilina had studied them, the same as she'd studied everyone else, but that was no real help. Jindarians had little by way of weaknesses. Yes, she had trained in some of their fighting techniques, so should be able to repel a hand-to-hand assault, but that wouldn't stop Keily from lining them up in her sights and taking them out. Although she wondered if the assassin had talked up her skills to Mandine. After all, she still hadn't killed her target, after three attempts. Maybe she was better at boasting than shooting.

But she had still managed to find them several times so Misilina couldn't write her off. And without the safety zone, Misilina was next to useless. Nothing she had in her head would give her muscles the strength and speed they needed to defeat a Jindarian even if Keily's abilities were so-so.

Misilina ran through every single thing she'd learnt about them, turning each precious lesson over in her head like the most valued memories, listing everything in her mind and going over it again and again and again—

'So where are they?'

She blinked as her attention was drawn back to Jolan. 'What?'

'These other places that have sugar. Where are they?'

She crouched in a shadow and turned to him. 'There are two in less than a maxispan or so based on our current speed. One is a small depot for local ground transports that offers cold beverages to the drivers who move goods in and out. The other is a storage facility that supplies various items used for Darsairian celebrations, you know, like their fertility day and death day, jewel day and when they worship their sand god, Darsin.'

'And they have sugar drinks?'

'Yes. Not much, I grant you. This facility usually stocks larger things like stands and stages, decorative poles. The drinks are just for any customers coming to place an order. Fortunately, Darsairians enjoy sugar as much as most races that look like us. That's why it wasn't on the major list. Its stores are insignificant. Enough for me, though.' Hopefully.

'Hm.' Jolan stroked his chin and some life re-entered his eyes. No, it was more than that. It wasn't a noble squaring-of-the-shoulders-and-moving-on kind of glance. This was a look she remembered all too well from her childhood. Every time he planned a prank. That look struck more fear in her heart than Keily did.

'What?' she said.

'I think that's our best bet,' he said. 'How do we get in there?'

'They have a triple-rated security badge. Getting in without my comm unit isn't impossible, but it will be tricky. No matter which way we try to get in, we'll set off an alarm. That wouldn't normally be an issue, as I could take out the automated security bots easily and crowd control would likely take too long to get there. We'd be out by then. But while Keily may not be close enough to reach us in time, she might be. It's a huge risk.'

'Not if we have a distraction.'

'A distraction?' This couldn't be good.

He nodded past her. 'Look, there's a clothing manufacturer. Do you know what kind of security they have?'

'Um ...' She hadn't paid much attention to clothing facilities. 'Just a basic level by the looks of it.'

'Good. Let's break in.'

'Why?'

He smirked. 'Trust me.'

How many times had she heard that before? When they'd broken into the throne room during renovations so they could sit on his parents' thrones. She hadn't wanted to and even once she had been there she couldn't bring herself to sit on Lady Talma's throne, but that had made no difference when her father had stripped her of privileges for a week. Then there was the time that Jolan had dared her to shinny down the side of the palace wall from three levels up. The fall could have killed her. Two weeks of no privileges.

She wasn't putting up with it this time. 'You tell me why first.'

'We need to look like locals. That way we'll blend in more.'

That made a little sense. The manufacturer made mining wear, so if they could dress simply, they would look like locals going about their business. They weren't as angular-looking as the average Darsairian, but most people probably wouldn't notice from a quick glance, especially since the clothes themselves, designed for angular bodies, would help. She should have thought of that herself. But it sounded a bit too sensible for Jolan.

It was a moment's work to slip the simple energy lock on the door and go inside. Misilina grabbed some garments that looked about her size and put them on, making a note of everything they took. She would make sure the Agency recompensated the business for what they'd lost. She considered taking her jumpsuit with her, as it had a built-in belt designed to hold sugar canisters, but it would be too awkward to carry and she knew that the canisters she found in Tekkon would be unlikely to fit anyway. She could slip them in the oversized pockets at first and try and rig up a belt system later.

Since her old suit was virtual, she clicked on the shoulder and it faded into nothing. No need to leave evidence behind. It was a pity she didn't have her comm unit. If she had, she could have produced another one when she needed it, and adjusted the belt as well.

Unfortunately, given Jolan's position, his clothes weren't virtual. She would have to dump them somewhere.

Jolan rummaged through rack after rack before he settled on something. To her surprise, he opted for darker ones that wouldn't stand out. All scarily appropriate choices. *What's he planning?*

Once he was done, he looked her up and down. 'Yeah, that'll do.'

He headed for the door. As much as she wanted to take him to task there and then, she knew they needed to get out as soon as possible. She would quiz him once they were safe.

She grabbed his clothes, dumping them a short distance away. In the darkness of the nearest alley, she turned to him, arms folded. 'So what's all this for?'

But he turned his head left and right, seeking something. His eyes lit up. She heard it too—the distant chatter of a large group of people coming close. Rebels.

She tugged at his hand. 'This way.'

But he stood firm. 'No. *This* way.'

He pulled her towards the sound and she stuck her heels in. 'Are you crazy? That's a mob. They'll rip us apart. You'll be killed.'

'Not dressed like this we won't.' He picked up some filth from the gutter at their feet and smeared it on his face. 'Come on. We need to look the part.'

He'd lost his mind. The stress of Mandine's betrayal must have fractured it. 'Jolan, you can't just walk straight into a mob of rebels. If they recognise you, you're dead. And if they don't recognise you, crowd control might kill you with the rest of them. Do you really think they're not going to take action against anyone seen with these people?'

'You want to get into that storage facility, don't you?' He pointed towards the sound. 'That's the perfect way to do it.'

'Are you kidding? Do you know how much attention that will attract? Everyone will see it!'

'Exactly. Keily isn't going to think we're in the middle of a huge scene, is she?'

She frowned. 'No, but crowd control—'

'They're dealing with this kind of thing all over the city. What are the chances that they'll target this one?'

'If you make them loot a storage facility they will!'

He shrugged. 'If they get there in time. We'll just have to be fast.'

He started walking towards the sounds of the rabble before she could stop him. She raced to catch up. 'Jolan, you're being ridiculous!'

'If you've got a better idea, you can mention it.'

She didn't have a better idea. But that was hardly the point. Did he even realise what he was suggesting? He was a member of the High Family of Verindon and he was going to incite a riot in order to break into a facility. 'Do you know what this could do to your family's reputation? To the whole *planet's*? That you could be seen to be part of something like this … you can't do it.'

He pulled up and turned to face her. 'But it's fine if just the two of us break in and steal stuff, is it?'

She could feel her anger mounting. 'That's different.'

He glared at her. 'I'm listening. Why?'

It should have been obvious. 'Breaking in to steal a few small items to keep us alive in an enemy environment is standard training practice for agents under section B code twenty-five.'

He waved a dismissive hand and started walking again. 'I'm sick of your codes. It's no different.'

'It *is* different! A mob that size could destroy the entire facility. Wreck everything. Ruin livelihoods. If there happen to be workers in there, they could kill them. And I know Darsairian law. Rioters doing something like that are in danger of execution. Are you going to ask all of them to risk their lives for you? No, of course not. You're not going to tell them the risks. You can't.'

She could hear the scorn rising in her tone and was sure he could too. But it didn't stop him. 'You think these people haven't been doing this all night? They're already facing death. It won't stop them. I'm just … going to channel their fury to our benefit.'

Unbelievable. 'Yes, I guess that's something you've always been good at, letting someone else take the fall for your pranks.'

He stopped short and turned back to face her. She watched the emotions flit across his face. He was angry. He was hurt. *Like he had any reason to be.* He was scornful. He was …

Reflective? Was that what it was?

But he set his mouth. 'Come on.'

She groaned. She could hardly order him to stop. And she couldn't let him go alone. She raced after him, scooping some mud from the path and smearing it onto her face and clothes.

At the next turn he started running. She saw why. The mob was passing the mouth of the street. There must have been at least sixty of them. He hurried to join them, Misilina just behind.

Some miners, men and women both, saw them and smiled in welcome. 'Come on! We're going to attack Mining Central!' She was glad she understood their language enough to make sense of their words.

Fortunately, so did Jolan. He let out a whoop and raced along with them, yelling epithets in Darsairian and snarling along with those around him, growling his agreement at their outraged protests. He slowed momentarily to let her draw beside him. 'Are we going the right way to get to that facility?'

She nodded. 'It's to the left a few streets down.'

'Let me know when it's in sight.'

Would they be able to see it from there? Maybe a little. She kept her eyes on each junction they passed, scanning for the right building. Jolan moved them to the left of the mob.

As they reached the intersection, she tugged on his arm and he halted, several people behind him nearly running into him. 'Hey,' he said, his voice ringing out over the hubbub, 'isn't that where they keep those things for the Jewel Celebration? We should go there,' he shouted in almost perfect Darsairian. 'Then we can decorate Mining Central. Remind them who really does all that work and makes the celebrations possible. They don't care that they get to celebrate off *our* hard work, off *our* bent backs. We need to *show* them who deserves to be celebrated!'

If there was one thing Jolan knew how to do, it was to create a presence. The miners hung off every word, murmuring agreement, the murmuring growing into a rumbling, and then into a roar.

'Decorate Mining Central!'

'Let's make them *see* who we are!'

'They need to know we won't stand for this treatment anymore!'

Jolan was at the head of the crowd as they surged down the street towards the storage facility, urging them on, his face eager, until they overtook him and reached the gate ahead of him. Misilina tried to stay by his side the whole way, but the crowd had made him their champion and it was hard to keep up. But as they moved past him and stormed the gate, he stepped back and she was able to grab his shoulder. 'Get back. Don't be involved in this.'

'We need to be involved. You've got to get what you need before they destroy everything.'

She'd been afraid of this.

The crowd had trouble with the fence, as they couldn't break through the power lines with brute force. But it seemed they'd already encountered that problem during their evening of rioting, as they waved one of their women forward. She stepped up, an electronic device in her hands. It only took a few moments before she had deactivated the fence and it disappeared.

The barrier removed, the miners raced forward with cries of glee and began pounding on their next obstacle—a metal door. This one could only be removed by brute force, but they had enough of that to go around, some of them racing to different points in the yard and returning with posts from some old machinery in a corner. They threw everything they had at the door, including themselves, until it buckled, making a gap in the side. The female miner again came forward, slipped through the hole and with a grind of machinery, the warped door slid aside as far as it could. It was far enough for the miners to push through, taking the rest of the door off as they did.

Misilina grabbed Jolan and rushed in, past the security bots, which the woman had powered down. Fortunately, Misilina knew exactly where to go. Getting there would be the tricky part as the miners spread throughout the facility, tearing displays down, breaking open cabinets and storage cupboards, pulling out everything they could find. Some used diggers to destroy the merchandise, others covered themselves with streamers and danced around, the shiny coloured metal strips catching in the streetlight that streamed through the destroyed door.

She pushed her way through the rioting miners, finally finding a small cabinet that someone had just started to pry open. Eager hands were waiting to take the sugar-laden drinks. Misilina forced herself to the front.

There were shrieks and squeals as the cabinet broke. Misilina snagged three cans, while Jolan nabbed two for her. He got into a tugging match with a female miner who snarled at him, wild-eyed. 'That's for *me*. You've already got one!'

He wrenched it out of her hand and Misilina grabbed his sleeve before the woman could throw the punch she was lining up. 'Come on.'

But Jolan wouldn't let her just race out. He picked up some abandoned streamers and draped them around them both, handing over the cans of sugary drinks in the process. Misilina stuffed them into the large pockets on her miner's trousers. She tried to hitch up the pants while snarling at Jolan. 'What are you doing?'

'Playing our roles. Or do you think they won't notice if we just hurry out of here and disappear?'

She realised he was right—they were being stared at. Had someone recognised him? She tried to act as though she was taking part and enjoying the mayhem, but they had achieved their objective and they needed to vacate the premises as quickly as possible and plan their next move. Anything else was a waste of time.

She gritted her teeth as he spun her under his arm, then felt her face heat up when he placed his hands on her hips, pulling her closer as if they were dancing. That was definitely wrong. Definitely. Absolutely. She couldn't look at him.

To her amazement, her body began to move with his, closer, almost against her will. *Get your mind back on your job.* Enough of this foolishness! She began to manoeuvre them towards the door. Jolan came willingly, dancing and twirling her all the way. Why couldn't he stop that?

Why didn't she want him to?

'Come on, loosen up, Missy. You used to love dancing when you were little.'

Don't call me Missy! 'In case you hadn't noticed, I'm not little anymore.'

Finally, they were at the door and made their way through the miners who had come to join the party. A few were in the yard, some in corners engaging in … well, Misilina wasn't going to look too closely but the blood rose to her face again.

Jolan shrugged. 'At least they're having fun.'

Fun? It was so hard not to yank him out of there and pull him down the street, but she had to remember his position and her own. As they got further away from the facility, her rage finally exploded. 'You call that fun? That was nothing to do with fun! That was a ploy to get what we needed, nothing more.'

He was nonchalant. 'And it worked, didn't it?'

'At the expense of someone's business,' she hissed. 'At the expense of getting those people killed. Jolan, for once can't you think of the consequences of your actions?'

They hadn't even made it into the shadows but he stopped anyway, his feet sliding together and grinding to a halt. He turned furious eyes to her. 'That's what you think of me? An entitled brat who never thinks about anything but himself?'

The force of his glare took her by surprise. She caught a glimpse of something behind it, but she couldn't grasp what it was. 'What am I supposed to think? Look what you just did!'

He stepped closer, the anger writ large on his face. 'Misilina, I don't know if you noticed, but you didn't have a clue how to get the sugar you need in order to keep us both alive. I just did that for you. The least you can do is be grateful, rather than complain about how it happened.'

'Grateful.' She wanted to hurl abuse at him but sounds on the street brought her back to reality. 'Come on, we need to get off the street.'

She thought he wasn't going to follow, but she heard an exasperated sigh before he began to stride after her. After that she kept them moving for as long as possible. They needed to put a considerable distance between themselves and the scene of the riot. Not to mention that, as long as she was thinking about her assignment, it stopped her from berating him.

She could imagine the conversation. *I'll tell him the truth. He is entitled. He is a brat. He doesn't think before he acts. He doesn't even think after he acts!* She didn't think he meant any harm, but there was no excuse for reckless endangerment, especially from a member of the high family.

Eventually, she had to pull her mind off him and back on the task at hand. At least they had sugar now. The next step was to find a weapon of some kind, possibly a communication device at the same time. She had already run through a list of potential locations but breaking into a weapon store was going to be a lot more of a challenge than finding sugar. There were limited options … officially, anyway. *Will Keily know about the unofficial sources?*

Some residents kept armaments for themselves, even though they weren't allowed to. Then there was the crime element of Tekkon. She ruled them out; they wouldn't give up their weapons willingly, and Keily would definitely know about them. Although, there would be some small operators in the seedier parts of town. Small-time criminals and the like. It should be easy enough to take on one of them. She might not even need to go into the safety zone. It wasn't the best plan—taking Jolan there was an appalling risk, and she could hardly leave him behind.

His voice broke through her plotting. 'Are you going to tell me the plan or do you think I'm too irresponsible to handle something like that?'

Her irritation flared up again. She tried to stamp on it before she opened her mouth. *Father would keep himself under control. Breathe out.* There. She could at least look him in the eye without screaming at him now. 'We need to find weapons. I think I've got a good idea where we could find one or two. Not many, but it's better than nothing.'

His eyes darted between hers, dissecting her expression. 'You think you can find ... Straight back to business, of course. And here I thought you were going to rage and scream and rant. I should have known better.' He sat down in the gutter, making sure to stay out of the light.

What? She had just spent time deliberately trying to calm herself down and he wanted to go at it again? She spun to face him. 'You want to tell me I'm wrong or stupid or not good enough at all this, go ahead. Just keep your voice down so no one passing hears us.'

That jolted him. His mouth dropped open. 'I don't want to say any of that.'

Good. Then they could move on. 'So you want to hear what we're going to do next?'

'No, Missy!' At least he was hissing under his breath. 'I want you to acknowledge that I'm not a total idiot, some unhelpful elite fool you've been stuck with who does nothing but get under your skin.'

'You do get under my skin. You drive me insane. It happens all the time.'

'Because you think I'm entitled.'

'You *are* entitled, Jolan! You have every privilege anyone could want. The only people your age with more are your two brothers and your sister, and that's only because they're further along in the line of succession than you. And you were prepared to bond with a woman you didn't love, who clearly wasn't exactly the charity lover you were—'

'I get that, okay? I get that.' He put his head in his hands.

Misilina sucked in a breath. How could she be so cruel, reminding him of the fact that the woman he was going to bond with clearly preferred it if he was dead? And why? Why had Mandine wanted to bond with him if she only intended to kill him?

But her agent-like thinking melted away at the sight of him. The defeat in him.

He didn't lift his head. Were his shoulders shaking? He … he wasn't crying, was he?

A long-buried memory resurfaced of Jolan aged seven, slumped in a corner, crying because he couldn't go to Cress' junior graduation because he hadn't scored high enough in his exams. She could still hear his voice. *'But I tried so hard, Missy.'*

She had reached out to him, all of five years old, and given him a hug. *'There, there,'* she'd said. *'There, there. I'll stay here and play, Jolan.'*

He'd put his arms around her and held her for a while.

Her fingers twitched, wanting to reach out. But how could she? He was no longer seven and she was no longer five. He was a leader, she an agent. But the tingling in her fingertips wouldn't go away. It turned to a burning, almost like her body was punishing her for failing to comfort a friend. It was a long time since she'd thought of him that way.

She rubbed her hands together to ease the pain. Distraction, that's what she needed. No more thinking like she was a child. 'Come on, we need to keep moving.'

He looked up, his eyes piercing hers. He *had* been crying. 'Sure.'

She led them further into the darkness, hearing his heavy step behind her. It seemed keeping them on the move wasn't enough of a distraction. And she had something else on her mind anyway. 'I wonder why she did it.'

He snorted. 'Yeah, let's talk about her strategy. That's bound to be helpful.'

'Well, I think it will help if we know what she's up to, don't you? Know your enemy.'

She could almost hear him smile. 'Your mother says that.'

She shrugged that off. 'They used to say it on Earth, apparently. Father says it's definitely something good to know.'

'Well, if *he* thinks that, it must be right.'

She glared at him in the dim light from a street globe nearby. 'What's that supposed to mean?'

'Nothing. You're right. We should try and work out why she did this. I mean, she obviously did it because I am a gullible fool, but that's not the real reason, I'm sure.'

She opened her mouth to discuss her theories, but his face stopped her. 'You're not gullible.'

He laughed derisively. 'Apparently, I am.'

'Jolan, you have advisors around you constantly and no one picked up on this. Not your parents, not mine, not High Commander Zaden. No one.'

'Yeah, but they didn't kiss her, did they? It's not the same.' Shoulders slumped, he kept walking. 'So do you have any idea why?'

'Well, you knew her best. Do you have any ideas?'

'No, not really. And it's not like I haven't been thinking about it. I mean, as I said earlier, she's shallow, but so's every girl in that circle. She runs charities, so I thought that meant she had some depth.'

'Yes, she gave that one to your mother.' Was there a reason for that?

'Yes, they shared that.' He shook his head. 'This is going to hit Mother so hard. She loved that Mandine was as passionate about charities as she was. She always complained that no other girl of that age had any real interest in that. I mean, they run them, but their hearts aren't in it.'

'None of them?'

Jolan looked up. He must have caught her tone. 'No, none. Why?'

Misilina thought about that. 'It's very much your mother's thing, isn't it?'

'It kind of goes with the job of being the consort.'

And there it was. The connection. 'No one else in elite circles does that. Well, they do, but they make it clear they don't really care about it. Mandine's a better actor, it seems.'

'So you think she acted it up to impress my mother? That wouldn't surprise me. But Mother can identify lies too, you know.'

'She can, but she's not the most skilled lie detector around. If Mandine was careful, she could get around that.'

'I guess so,' he conceded. 'So it was all an act to make my mother favour her?'

But that wasn't exactly where she was going. She tried to lead Jolan in the right direction, determined to tread gently this time. 'Yes, it's something Cress appreciates in her too, isn't it? Do any of the women on his list run charities?'

Jolan wasn't there yet. 'Yes, but it's all a show to them, and he doesn't have any interest in any of them anyway. You know Cress. He doesn't like frivolous girls. And he likes it if he can be the strong one. He loves to be the rescuer. You remember that from when we were kids, don't you? The way he was always the one to swoop in and save you and Tilla, Selli and Lina if you were stuck up trees or caught somewhere.'

She let a smile frame her face. 'Yes, because you left us there.'

He looked guilty. 'Well, I always knew he'd swoop in and save—'

She could tell when he got it. When everything clicked for him. 'No. No, that can't be the reason. Are you telling me that she only bonded with me to …'

It was hard seeing the pain on his face as he realised. 'As you said, he does love it when he can swoop in and save a girl.'

'But that makes no sense. She's not on his list. She barely made it onto mine. Why would she think she could get Cress?'

'Your parents have been known to bend the rules, haven't they? Why not do it for the grieving partner of their youngest son?' She regretted saying this as soon as the words were out because his face twisted into a mask of pain. Again, she felt the urge to reach out to him.

He grasped her fingers and she almost drew back in shock. She didn't realise her hand had stretched out to meet his. His hand entwined with hers and she didn't draw away. It felt strangely … good.

His eyes locked with hers for a long moment. What was it that made her do this? It must be the resurrection of their childhood connection. 'It's not your fault.' Even saying that was so unlike who she was trying to be.

He gave her a half-smile. 'It's all right. I think my ego is bruised more than anything else. That I let myself get drawn in. That I was duped. After all,' his gaze dropped to her lips. 'It's not like I loved her.'

Misilina felt strange. Her heart was beating fast. That woke her up. Whatever was going on, she couldn't let it distract her from her assignment. She needed to get Jolan home safely. But it was difficult disentangling her hand from his. It wanted to stay there.

She gently drew it back. 'We've got to keep going.' Something made her avoid his eyes. 'We've got to find a weapon and a communication device.'

'Two weapons.'

She looked up, puzzled. 'Why two?'

He rolled his eyes, but he looked more amused than offended. 'Come on, Missy. Give me some credit. I may not be able to go into the safety zone, but I do know a thing or two about defending myself. And if I'm the target in all this, then I need to be able to do that.'

That was fair enough. 'Okay. Follow me.'

CHAPTER THIRTEEN

Pravvit had been busy while they'd been trapping Councillor Veston into giving something away. When Sarah contacted him on her comm, he immediately downloaded several different compromising vids and files that told of a long trail of white-collar crime. It seemed that the councillor had been happy to employ anything he could in his desire to climb the social ladder. She didn't even need to visit Pravvit. Instead, she went straight to the interrogation room.

It wasn't often she went to the lower levels of the Agency headquarters. She had a lot of bad memories from her first few years on the planet, most involving those lower sections where criminals were quizzed for details, often tortured and sometimes mysteriously disappeared either before or after trials. She had last seen the man she had called uncle, who had tried to kill her to take the throne, in those very rooms. Later, he'd been moved to house arrest and was found dead below the balcony of his home. He wasn't a man for suicide.

Then, she had seen her adoptive mother, the woman who had raised her in her first few years on Earth, also encaged there, her sneering face forever burned into Sarah's memory as she had mocked her. Korviki was her real name, and her appearance set in motion the chain of events that had led to Sarah being removed from the throne of Verindon. Admittedly, it was this very act that had gained her the man she loved, but that didn't make the memories rosy. After all, it had nearly killed them both.

And here she was again, but this time the room didn't hold either

her arrogant uncle or her distant mother. The face she could see beyond the one-way glass was blanched in fear, eyes open wide in terror.

She stood beside Keridan where he watched the councillor, arms folded. He had just downloaded Pravvit's information into his comm. 'Interesting.'

'Should we threaten him with the Mind Warden?' Sarah asked.

Her bond-partner snorted. 'Why not? I don't think this will take long.' He opened the link between them and the room beyond. 'Councillor Veston?'

The man's face twitched, sweat streaming from every pore. 'Yes?'

'An examination of your financial records, both business and private, have revealed some interesting details about your life of riches and privilege. Would you care to explain these events to us or should we use the Mind Warden to fi—'

'No, please, anything but that! I couldn't ... Oh no. I'll tell you anything you want to know.'

Keridan broke the link and winked at Sarah. 'Knew it.' He shot a glance at the four guards who stood silently in the room with them. 'We're going in to interrogate the prisoner at close range. I doubt he's a threat to us, but two of you will also enter. You are to keep an eye on him. Watch for any suspicious actions.'

'Yes, Commander.'

He passed his hand over one of the lights on the console and the door slid open. The councillor didn't move from where he sat in the middle of the room, even though he was unrestrained. Clearly, he knew better than to make a fuss.

His chair was fixed to the floor, so remained turned towards the glass screen in front of him, but there was space for both Keridan and Sarah to stand in front of him. The other two agents who'd entered with them stood on either side of the prisoner.

Keridan knew how to make an impression. Sarah watched him carefully. She knew how it would go. First, he would fold his arms, then his eyes would glint. Steel would be in his voice, which would be strong and unwavering. The scars he'd gained when they'd defeated Traizon only added to his fierceness. Keridan knew how to employ them well.

Most of the effort would probably be wasted on Veston. Sarah knew he'd fold pretty quickly if even the words 'Mind Warden' made him beg for mercy.

Sure enough, his terrified eyes blinked up at Keridan, who took up his most threatening stance. 'Now, Councillor. I think you have some things to share with us. And please don't waste our time with lies.' He indicated Sarah. 'My bond-partner has already picked up a number from you. And any attempt to delay us with any kind of subterfuge or refusal to speak will be met with the harshest response.'

As Keridan's voice trailed off in a hiss, Sarah could see the councillor's knees knocking.

'It w-wasn't my idea.' Veston's eyes darted to Sarah. 'S-she can tell you that. It w-wasn't my idea at all. She *made* me do it. She's too ambitious, just like her mother!'

Sarah wasn't all that familiar with the councillor's family, given that they'd only come to prominence fairly recently, so had no personal experience with the councillor's deceased bond-partner. But what little she'd heard had screamed social climber of the worst kind—taking every opportunity for her own advancement regardless of who fell along the way, desiring the finest things in life regardless of cost, she had to be seen with the right people. It reminded her of the students at the prestigious school she'd attended on Earth—self-interested egomaniacs who wanted everything they could get to give themselves prominence, come hell or high water.

Keridan's gaze didn't waver. 'You're saying this was all Mandine's idea?'

Veston nodded furiously. 'She had to have everything. Her mother did too. Buying those mines, that was her idea.'

'Mandine's or your bond-partner? Ilicina, wasn't that her name?'

Again a rapid nod. 'She was like that from the day we bonded. Nothing was ever good enough for *her*. And she was lower born than me! Pushed me from day one to get more, get higher, be noticed. Always wanted the best things.

'Mandine was the same. I didn't see it at first—she was always such a good girl, so sweet and engaging. That was her way, you know. She would draw you in, then get what she wanted. By the time you knew what she was doing, it was too late.'

'And what did she want this time?' Sarah asked.

The councillor sniffed. 'She wanted to be a member of the high family.'

'She was about to become one,' Keridan said evenly. 'Wasn't that her goal?'

'Pah! To bond with the most junior member of that family? Someone like Jolan, who was never likely to amount to much? Always running around after a new girl? That's what made it easy for Mandine, you see, he wasn't hard to get. She just had to be flashy enough to catch his eye. Of course it worked; soon he was fawning all over her like a love-sick fool. Although …' Veston gave Sarah a thoughtful glance; not surprising, since she had just picked up the flicker of an untruth from him. 'I never knew if it was genuine in him either. Not like the men she usually had following her around. Sometimes he even looked positively bored. She didn't like that. That's what made it easy to betray him.'

'But why did she do it?' Sarah asked.

He looked at them, surprised. 'Isn't it obvious? Jolan wasn't enough for her. Never would be. She wanted Cress. She wanted to be consort— the highest woman in her generation. But there was no way she would ever get on his list. So what could she do to gain his attention? What might get them to make an exception for her?'

She and Keridan looked at each other. 'She planned to kill Jolan and then convince Cress to bond with her out of pity?' he said.

'Of course. Cress had already noticed her because of her charity work. She carefully selected her charities to mirror the ones Lady Talma ran. That got Mandine in good stead with *her*. She was sure Cress would follow. He's all about doing the right thing. He was bound to want to help her out.'

Sarah raised an eyebrow. While Mandine might have been able to dupe Talma to some extent, that was a long way from getting Ardon to agree to something like this, and he, as the overlord, would be the one who had the final say. Ardon the sceptical. Ardon the cynic. Ardon, who had seen through the false flutterings of many an eyelash in his day and had chosen Talma as his bond-partner. Why? Because she had a flicker of genuineness about her. If Mandine had really set her eyes on Cress, Ardon would have noticed that eventually. How could she even have expected to get past Talma for long, with her ability to identify lies?

Keridan's face was just as doubtful. 'I think your daughter was overselling her abilities.'

Veston shrugged. 'Probably. Like I said, too ambitious for her own good. But would she listen? No! Not to me. I told her she was asking too much. I said just bond with a second-tier councillor and let your children move further up. But no, it had to be *her*. She couldn't wait.' He looked at them hopefully. 'But you can bring her home, yes?'

Keridan was doubtful. '*If* she's still alive.'

'Oh, she will be.' Again the unshakeable confidence. 'Keily will make sure of that.'

Sarah frowned. 'Keily? Her lady-in-waiting?' She had seen the girl around but had paid little attention to her.

Veston puffed up with pride. 'She's not a lady-in-waiting. She's not even Verindonian. She's a highly trained assassin. It was her job to incite the miners to riot so we'd have someone to blame. Take out Jolan and as many of the agents as possible. She's a sniper, you see. She knows what she's doing.'

The horror on Keridan's face reflected Sarah's rising tide of despair.

Was there any chance that Jolan had survived? What about Misilina? What hope could a young girl, fresh out of the Academy, have of standing up under that kind of calculated attack? Their daughter was good, but …

It had been a while since that look had appeared on Keridan's face. His eyes fixed on the councillor; his nostrils flared. It was as if he was about to go into the safety zone. He bent over the man, putting his hands on the armrests of his chair, Veston shrinking back. 'So your daughter commissioned someone to kill not only someone in the line of succession but all his guards as well?'

'What about Mandine's guard?' demanded Sarah.

The councillor's frightened eyes shifted to her. 'She didn't mention them. I don't think she considered them a threat.'

Which meant it was likely they'd been eliminated. No, it couldn't be. Surely she would know if her daughter had died.

Keridan was calm, but his face was deadly. 'Councillor, thank you for that information. You will remain in a cell in isolation until we find out what has happened on Darsair.' Veston looked relieved until Keridan spoke again. 'This is for your own safety, of course. I'm sure you're aware that people who humiliate the Agency have long had a history of committing suicide.'

The councillor blanched. 'The Agency d-doesn't do things like that anymore.'

Keridan nodded. 'I hope so. But it hasn't been put to the test for a while.'

Veston glanced at Sarah with a pleading look on his face. 'Ambassador, you know I'm telling the truth. You know I had no choice. Don't let them do anything to me!'

Sarah had always been known for her compassion. She'd never been happy with the Agency's old habit of silencing people who shamed it. However, with her daughter in mortal danger and possibly dead, she wasn't in the mood to assuage Veston's fears. She shrugged delicately. 'I'm sure that's true, councillor. And I *think* you'll be safe. After all,

Agent Hajitis died over twenty years ago. If he were here now, I doubt you'd still be breathing.'

Veston looked equal parts relieved and disturbed. Keridan signalled to the two agents guarding Veston and they all left the room.

Once the door had slid shut behind them, Keridan turned to the guards. 'Take the councillor to a high-level cell and let me know its call number.'

The female guard glanced at her companion before turning her eyes back to Keridan. 'Does he make it there alive?'

Keridan's eyes glittered. 'The Agency doesn't do that anymore. There's a difference between psyching out a prisoner and murdering him. Moreover, he may have additional information we require. I expect him to reach his cell in perfect condition and stay that way.'

Sarah and Keridan marched out of the room together. It was a testament to her bond-partner's authority that Sarah had no doubt every command he'd given would be carried out to the letter. And although compassion flickered within her, she couldn't deny that part of her wanted to rip the councillor to shreds. 'So that was psychological warfare?'

He took her hand as they walked along. 'Killing him will achieve nothing. Even if Misilina is dead,' she heard his slight hesitation to say their daughter's name, 'you would never forgive yourself if you were involved in something like that, and you know it.'

She sighed. 'Yes, I daresay you're right. But I also really wish Hajitis was still alive. I can imagine how he'd react to this.'

Keridan laughed mirthlessly. 'Actually, you never saw him at his worst and I don't think you could have stomached it if you had. He enjoyed killing a little too much. If you knew the things he'd done ...'

She knew that Hajitis had delighted in violence. That's why she'd been afraid of him. But Keridan had never let her know all the details of the hits he'd carried out over the years. It had been a long time before Keridan had confessed that it was Hajitis who had murdered her uncle, having requested special permission from High Commander

Denzik to do it. He still wouldn't tell her exactly what the big agent had done, but even he had shivered when he'd talked about it, and he'd seen enough in his time that he should have been able to shrug it off.

'So what do we do now?' she asked.

'We try and get the Darsairian government to allow us to land in Tekkon. Now that we have some evidence, hopefully, they'll give in without a fight.'

'I'm going too.'

He smiled. 'Of course you are. We'll both go and take Pravvit and Perisina with us, and a few other agents of high standing.'

'David and our Hajitis will probably want to come too.' The boys would want to help save their sister if it was possible to do so.

'No. We need to do this as cleanly and efficiently as possible. Only the most experienced agents will come with us. I'll find out everything I can about Keily, see what her skills are.' He turned and took her in his arms. 'Misilina may not have survived, but if she has, there's no doubt that she'll be with Jolan, if he's still alive. And I know our daughter. I know what her every move is likely to be. I'm confident we'll be able to find her once we get there.'

She pulled him close. 'And hopefully in time to save them.'

CHAPTER FOURTEEN

It took Misilina a while to overcome the cautious part of her that said she couldn't take Jolan to Tekkon's underground district. Although she knew a lot about it, it was nothing more than information she'd found in the many files and searches she'd made into every facet of life in Tekkon. It stood her in good stead now, but it would still only go so far.

So there they were, hiding in the shadows, trying to keep out of the slurry that lined the filthy streets around them. Tekkon's underground wasn't far from the biggest mine, and the dross left over as the gems were refined had spilled out onto the streets. It was thick black muck with a smell that set her nose on fire. The cheap stone walls, uneven and worn, were stained a multitude of dark colours from the smoke that poured out of the refineries. She could feel it under her hands as she edged along the wall.

She sighed. Simply being in this environment could kill Jolan and she hadn't even come across a weapon yet.

He was right beside her, copying her every move—staying in the shadows, treading lightly and carefully on the uneven pavers beneath their feet.

She held up a hand, signalling for him to stop, as they reached a corner. She peered around it. The next street was empty, but further up at an intersection she could see what she had been looking for—a rough gem dealer. They inhabited the areas near the mines, stealing or finding offcut gems and polishing them up as finely as they could get them. They occasionally managed to swipe the good stuff as well, which made the Tekkon government come down hard on them, keeping them to dead-end areas like this one.

A Darsairian leant against the wall at the end of the street, smoking on an edge pipe, the wire coming out of his mouth and connecting to his pocket as he breathed in the dark fumes. Misilina knew that the downtrodden of Tekkon used the edge pipes to stave off hunger, keeping them in a semi-tranquil state. Luckily for them, it was getting near morning, and this man had clearly been smoking the pipe for some time if the way he lolled against the wall was anything to go by. There was a small humpy by his feet, a rough construction where he probably spent most of his time ... at least until they moved him on.

She turned back to Jolan. 'It would probably be best if you stay here.'

'You need someone to guard your back.'

She'd guessed he would say that. And why argue about it? He had some experience with self-defence. She was going to try and avoid going into the safety zone, and her target's dozy posture meant it was unlikely to be a problem. So why should she insist he stay where he was? 'We're looking for gems, the best he's got. I'll ask him, then when he reaches for the merchandise, I'll restrain him and look for weapons.'

'Why don't I ask him? That way you can be in a better position to attack.'

Why not indeed? She waved him forward with her.

They strolled around the corner, immediately catching the man's eye. He pushed himself off the wall and shoved his pipe in his pocket, spitting some liquified fumes into the gutter.

Jolan sauntered like a professional, with just the right amount of swagger and a touch of eagerness. He stopped a couple of handspans from the man and gave him a nonchalant look. 'What've you got?'

The man couldn't have been more than a few years older than her, Misilina thought, despite the lines on his face. His bushy eyebrows met together in the middle over misty eyes. She sidled closer to him, a little behind. He glanced at her but seemed too out of it to understand what she was doing.

'Best gems ever,' he said in a gruff voice. 'Cut as brilliant as you like.' He gave Misilina a lopsided grin. 'Present for the lady?'

She grabbed him by the neck, pinning him to the wall with her hand. 'We're not interested in gems.'

With a flick of his wrist, a knife came up, slicing at her arm. She yelped as the blade cut into her. He took advantage of that to step away, also producing a laser, a high grade one, by the look of the power cell. 'Nice try, but I'm not that easy.'

Good. Two weapons at least. But now she was going to have to use the safety zone. She would rather not, but they couldn't waste time. She zoned instantly, her target's eyes exploding wide at the sight. She wondered if he'd ever seen it before.

In the zone, it was the work of a microspan to grab the wrist with the knife and break it, wrenching the blade free in the process. He didn't even have time to fire the gun before a kick spun it out of his hand. Jolan retrieved it, wiping the dross from it and looking it over.

'Anything else?' she asked. She could see him shaking as her transformed face came close to his, her low slurred voice making him whimper.

'Please don't take my gems,' he begged.

'I don't care about your gems.' But she sensed there was something else. She reached around behind him. Stuffed into the back of his pants was a smaller, more compact laser. 'That'll do.' She shoved him against the wall before glancing at Jolan. 'Let's go.'

If she hadn't been in the safety zone, it would have been the end, but her senses alerted her and she dived to the side, tackling Jolan to the ground. She was never sure which one of them had been the target, but it didn't matter. She only noticed the burn mark as the shot singed the wall behind them.

Another shot rang out, taking out the Darsairian, and Misilina hauled Jolan to his feet and dived behind the humpy with him just before a blast exploded on the wall behind them.

At least she had cover now, although it wasn't much. It buckled as a shot hit it, but it was made from leftover metal sheets, so resisted the blast and left her with a convenient hole for return fire. She couldn't see her attacker, but it made no difference. She was still zonal, so she could tell where she was shooting from.

How good was the Darsairian's laser? Time to find out. She allowed her senses to line up Keily, who seemed to be on the move—seeking a better vantage point, no doubt—and fired. She heard it strike something; her senses told her she'd struck flesh.

'Move!' They had to get out while Keily checked her injury. There wasn't much cover in the rest of the street and the humpy wouldn't last forever.

They leapt to their feet and bolted for the shadows, Misilina keeping herself between Jolan and Keily. She could feel another blast coming. Would they make it in time?

They reached the corner and turned, launching into the darkness there, just as another shot rang out. Misilina felt a stabbing pain in her upper arm, not far from where the knife had nicked her. 'Keep moving!'

They didn't stop, even as the disturbing truth kept circling in her mind. Keily couldn't have known where they were. The odds of her picking Misilina's target were astronomical. How had she known?

The pain shot up her arm into her neck. She clamped her hands on the burn. Jolan must have realised as he stopped and turned to her. 'You've been hit!'

The pain of it made the safety zone fade away. 'What have you got on you?' she demanded.

He looked at her, uncomprehending. 'What?'

'She *has* to be tracking us. What could she be using? Did Mandine ever give you anything? Something small maybe.'

He was lost for a moment before understanding made his eyes

heavy with realisation. He reached into his pocket and pulled out a tiny chip. It was multicoloured and shone with rainbow light in the darkness.

'I forgot about this. She gave it to me just before we left, so I would remem—'

Misilina snatched it out of his hand and smashed it against the wall. 'We need to move.' Fortunately, he didn't argue.

Misilina used every bit of training she had to stagger their pattern so Keily couldn't find them. She kept both of them moving, staying in darkness where they could, until they approached the centre of the city again. She could soon hear the sound of riots. 'We can get lost in the crowds.'

Her arm was like a dead weight now, dragging her to the ground with its pulsing intensity. She had only felt virtual laser bolts before, as part of her training. She would have to tell the instructors to dial up the level of pain in their simulations. Nothing had prepared her for the shooting sensation that raced up her arm, into her skull, with every beat of her heart.

They began to move amongst a small crowd of miners, trying to hide within the group. Misilina concentrated on putting one foot in front of the other, hoping that they had finally lost Keily. She couldn't be sure; after all, if she'd been tracking them all this time, she would have seen them loot the storage facility. Missy could only assume that the woman hadn't been able to take them down for some reason. Maybe her long-range scope hadn't been good enough. Maybe she'd wanted evidence of Jolan flouting so many laws.

Or maybe she'd just known there was plenty of time.

Jolan pulled her good arm around her shoulders. She looked at it as if it belonged to someone else. Then she realised why—her feet wobbled against the street, no longer able to hold her.

'We need to find somewhere to fix up your wound,' he said.

She puffed out her reply, 'We need to keep moving.'

'If she was still close, she would have killed us by now. We need to find somewhere, just for a few maxispans. It's nearly dawn, anyway. We can't stay out in the open.'

He was right about that. She scoured her memory for anywhere close by that could shelter them during the daytime. It was hard to make her mind work, to dig up the plan of the city that had come to her so clearly earlier. 'This way.'

They headed down a side street away from the miners who were distracted by something burning up ahead. She and Jolan were in a residential section that had been closed some time ago, probably on the pretext of being redeveloped. Each row of small dwellings had a windowed door entry and was quiet and empty.

It didn't take long to find one where the door had been forced aside, leaving a small gap. Jolan went in first, concerned someone else might be sheltering there. Once he'd checked, he reached out and helped her crawl in, her arm screaming a protest that was hard to ignore.

The interior was dark and musty, the smell of dust, rot and soot tingling her nose. Unlike Verindonian dwellings, these homes only had windows in the doors, no others. Misilina could make out little of the room given the tiny amount of light that came through the window from the dim street lighting outside, although Darsair's sun was starting to light the horizon. In a maxispan or so, things would be brighter.

She tried to force her eyes open. She needed to guard Jolan. She was his only point of defence. She couldn't fail him!

He was a dim figure in the darkness. She saw a movement she couldn't identify, then heard the sound of ripping. He was tearing off part of his miner's shirt. It took her a moment to realise why.

She felt his hands, gentle as a whisper, on her arm. 'I can't see much of this,' he said, 'but it would be a good idea to cover it as well as we can. It's a good thing this shirt is new. It should be relatively clean, at least on the inside.'

She clenched her teeth as he wrapped a swathe around her arm. 'Given the weapon she was likely to be using, the wound should be pretty well cauterised on its own,' she told him in a hurried breath. 'Hopefully, it will be okay.'

He sighed. 'I wish we had more than this. Something for the pain.'

'It's all right. I know these kinds of wounds. A few maxispans' rest should be enough.' But she couldn't sleep. She needed to ensure he was safe. 'Hopefully, I can do that while I stand guard ... or sit, in this case. I think I need to sit.' She gave a breathless laugh.

'Don't be ridiculous,' he said. 'I'm perfectly capable of guarding both of us. There's nothing left for Keily to use to track us, so we should be safe here, and it's not like we're going to be able to move around much now that the sun's coming up anyway. We need to wait for night to fall again to make our next move.' His voice was like a caress. 'You can get all the rest you need.'

Her eyes felt like they were closing but duty wouldn't allow them. 'No, I need to—'

'Missy, lie down. You're about to fall asleep, you're so tired.' He put his arm around her and tugged her onto the floor, pulling her into his side, resting her head on his chest. A protest rose to her lips—this was hardly appropriate given his position and hers—but she couldn't get it out. She had no strength left for something as exhausting as speech.

In her last moments of consciousness, she felt something run over her hair. His hands? His lips? She couldn't tell, but it made her feel warm and safe. It was a false sense of security, like a dream, but it was nice. The voice of her agent side was buried under a wash of exhaustion and contentment.

CHAPTER FIFTEEN

Consciousness evaded her. She knew she was dreaming of Enyi dying beside her, dreaming of a sniper's bullets ringing out, agents falling, the panic of seeing Jolan in danger. It was too much. Her body wanted to thrash with the fear and grief of it, but something held her tightly. It settled and calmed her spirit. Whispered words soothed her and she slept, finally waking to a dull ache in her arm.

Her eyes squinted at the weak light that had invaded the dilapidated room. This had once been a residential dwelling, but now she could see it in the light, it was clear no one had touched the place in years. The Tekkon government had said they had already renovated and improved all the miners' dwellings, but her eyes told her otherwise.

The floor under her was hard and cold. Stone from one of the mines, probably. The walls were made out of cheap plastic slats. They had holes in various places, probably chewed by the small vermin that were native to this planet. There was no furniture, and as she'd noted a few maxispans earlier, only one window, in the door. It wasn't clear glass and only a limpid light of dark orange sun came through it.

She rolled over, stiff down one side, careful to make sure her throbbing arm didn't connect with the hardness of the floor, to find herself face to face with Jolan.

He gazed back at her, concern etching deep lines in his brow. 'How are you feeling?'

She went to sit up, but his arms around her made that difficult. She pressed her arm against the floor and found that the cold soothed it. That alerted her to the other aches that ran through her body, a testament to the hard floor that had been their bed.

Their bed. That thought woke her up a little more. Jolan had clearly slept beside her, holding her for however long she'd been asleep. With a grimace, he pulled his arm from under her head and massaged it. 'I'm glad you're awake. That was getting sore.'

Again, she tried to sit up. Again, his arms imprisoned her. She was sure she could have easily fought her way free but didn't feel like it, though it was embarrassing and highly inappropriate.

Then why couldn't she bring herself to care?

He seemed relieved to see her awake. 'How long have I been asleep?'

'About four maxispans, I think. I didn't have anything to keep track. Their sun appeared about a half a maxispan after you drifted off and I've been watching the movement of the light.' He pointed at the twinkle of brightness on the window. 'I know their days are a few maxispans shorter than ours and it's already late in the day their time, so I'm guessing a while. I slept a little too, so I'm not all that sure.'

He had fallen asleep also, leaving them both vulnerable. She shouldn't have left a civilian and a member of the high family to guard her. It was completely unacceptable. But her arm sent another throb through her, reminding her of why she'd needed to sleep. At least they'd survived their nap without being slaughtered.

He glanced at her arm. 'How is it?'

She sat up gingerly and this time he let her move, sitting up beside her. 'I think it's feeling a little better.' The throb, although still intense, was not the burning agony it had been the night before. She unwrapped his makeshift bandage and was pleased to see that the flesh, while black and broken, was not streaked with red. She felt she would recover sooner rather than later. She would just have to endure a sore arm for a few days.

He seemed relieved. 'I'm glad to hear it. You cried out a lot. I was worried it might be worse than you originally thought.' His face looked stricken, even though he tried to smile. 'I was a little worried that you wouldn't wake up at all.'

'I wouldn't do that to you,' she said, blushing as she realised how that came out. What would he think of her? 'I mean, you're my assignment. I need to see you back to Verindon safely. I'm not going to leave you to face this alone.'

His face, which had lit with delight at her words, slowly dulled. 'That's right. I'm just a job to you.'

What did he mean by that? 'That's all you can be.'

He ran his finger along a crack between the floor stones. 'What if it wasn't that way?'

She wasn't sure she'd heard him right, given how low his tone had been. 'What do you mean?'

He shrugged. 'Maybe a better thing to say is why do you think that? I mean, we grew up together. Your family, my family, they've always been close.'

Why were they even having this conversation? 'What does that have to do with anything?'

He sat back, frustration clear on his face. 'You'll never get it.'

'What?' He couldn't be saying ... She was a newly graduated agent. He was in the line of succession. The idea that something could happen between them was ridiculous, even if their families were close.

Then why was her mind searching for reasons he could be right?

His eyes pierced hers sharply, dissecting every expression on her face. 'You certainly got some skills from your mother, though.'

Her mind rebelled against the idea. 'Barely.'

'Tell me then—how did you know that Mandine would betray us?'

She frowned. 'I didn't.'

He silenced her with a shake of his head. 'Before you even went into that factory you knew something was up. I could tell by the look on your face. It wasn't just frustration with her, something had made you suspicious. What was it?'

She thought back to their visit to the factory to gain her sugar stores. In all the frantic rush of trying to keep him safe, she had forgotten the little word that had flashed through her mind when Mandine had spoken.

Lie.

'I—' she swallowed her words. One flash of insight didn't prove she was now a lie detector.

'And you didn't doubt me when I said I didn't love Mandine. Why? You had every reason to believe that was true.'

She snorted. 'Given how many girls you've cycled through over the past few years that wasn't a huge stretch.'

He cocked his head. 'Jealous?'

Her face heated up. Probably from amazement. 'What reason would I have to be jealous?' Why was her voice so high and squeaky?

His face was serious and direct. 'You can tell when people are lying. You may not have been able to do it before, but you can now.'

'That's purely conjecture.'

'Okay then, let's test it. I love Mandine.'

Lie. The word clanged in her head again. She didn't want to admit what had just happened. This was going somewhere and it filled her body with angst. She didn't want him to say it. She didn't want to know—

'I love you.'

She waited for the response, for the sign that it was untrue, for the flicker that would strike her spirit and reveal he was lying.

Nothing happened.

She buried her face in her hands, wincing as her arm ached. 'That's a lie.'

'No, it's not.'

'It is.'

'It's not and you know it.'

'It has to be.'

He reached up and gently tugged on her hands, pulling them away from her face. 'Missy, I love you. I've loved you for years.'

'And yet you always had a girl on your arm!' *Watch it, Misilina!* She was way too emotional.

'Because I didn't think I had a chance at you.'

'Because you are a Verindal. I am a Vendel.' Well, not really. She was *almost* a Vendel. Her mother's Verindal blood ran through her veins, tainting her with the status of crossbreed. 'Verindal and Vendel aren't allowed to bond with each other.'

He stroked his chin thoughtfully. 'Before your parents.'

'My mother was more than half-Vendel by the time they'd bonded.'

'Still, she has Verindal blood.'

'But,' she countered, 'the ruling against bondings between our two races still exists.'

'Actually, it's more specifically the high family,' he said. 'You know, no bonding with an overlord.'

'There still haven't been any interracial bondings since my parents.'

He didn't seem to be listening, pondering almost to himself, 'And the only reason that law is still there is because they haven't had any reason to deal with it.'

She pursed her lips. 'Then what was the problem? If you feel this way, if you really *believe* we could ...' She couldn't form the words. 'Why only mention it now?'

'Because you never paid any attention to me.'

Ha! 'I followed you around for years, let you lead me into all kinds of trouble. I was always getting punished for the things you talked me into doing. And I paid an enormous amount of attention when you set my hair on fire!'

He groaned and pushed away from her. 'Misilina, I was *twelve*!'

'I was *ten*!'

'I didn't mean to do it. You've no idea how bad I felt.'

'You're right. I have no idea. You didn't look too upset about it at the time.' Neither had his father.

'You didn't see the punishment I got when I got home. I lost privileges for weeks. Father was not happy. Not that I cared, of course. I felt so terrible about what I'd done I would have taken anything. For the next week, I asked him how you were every day.'

That took her by surprise. The vision of Overlord Ardon rocking back and forth with tears of laughter streaming down his cheeks was one of her strongest memories of the day, that and Jolan's nonchalant shrug. She couldn't look at him. 'But you didn't say anything.'

'I didn't know what to say.' He crept closer. 'Especially since, when I came back, you were so distant. We didn't have fun anymore. We didn't do the things we used to. It was like I'd lost you.'

The devastation in his voice made her raise her eyes to his as he continued. 'It didn't help that one of Father's conditions was that I do better in my schooling. I was determined to show him I could be a success. Determined to show you ... But you hardly ever looked at me again. You turned your mind to your training and that was that. I didn't know how to get you back.'

Could it really be true? Could this confession, this revelation, be real? But it had to, didn't it? If she could now tell when people were lying, then she would know if this was untrue. The clang of falseness should sound in her head. But there was nothing. Just silence.

His hands formed gentle manacles around her wrists. 'I know I'm not good enough for you. I know that I can't be an agent. I know that, if you did care anything for me, you could never produce energy with me the way your parents can, because I *am* a Verindal, full-blooded. And I know that you might hesitate because of the way some people have treated you because you have both Vendel and Verindal blood. But honestly, Misilina, I can't stop it. I love you so much. And if you decide you don't want me, I'll understand. I'll stay away. But we're here and we're together and you're listening to me for the first time in years. I couldn't stop myself from trying.'

It couldn't be true. It couldn't be real. And what was he asking her to decide? To accept him? To be with him? Despite the prestige of his family, he was right—it wouldn't be easy. Even if his parents accepted them on a personal level, they were the rulers of the planet. He had still been given a list of eligible women to choose from, all Verindal. No one would be expecting it.

And what would it lead to? Ridicule for her. For him. For their families. For any family they had together. Could she cope with that? How could she?

And her training? What would this mean for her future? She was an agent! That was all she'd wanted to be for years. Would it mean she would have to give that up?

Why was she even considering this? It made no sense. She was a rule keeper, a stickler for detail, the one who made sure the tiniest guideline was followed. If it hadn't been for her parents ignoring the rules, she wouldn't have mixed blood.

But no matter how hard she tried to view it dispassionately, to think of the rules, to think with the mind of an agent, still her heart beat faster at his shy expression, with a half-smile as he glanced up. She couldn't deny that it pleased her to see him look at her that way. She couldn't stop her hands from trembling at his gentle touch.

She couldn't love him. It was against everything she'd ever believed in!

But she didn't move away. She didn't firmly clamp down on his enthusiasm. She couldn't bring herself to destroy his hope. And when he crept nearer and nearer, she didn't stop him.

He placed his hand against her cheek, shaping it to her face. She tingled at his warmth.

His mouth came closer to hers. 'Missy ...'

The touch of his lips on hers was so gentle, so soft that she couldn't still the tremble that ran throughout her body. She knew he'd felt it as his arm snaked around her waist, drawing her closer. He held her face fast to his, kissing her gently, and laid her back down on the stone beneath them, his body above hers. His warmth enveloped every part of her, so she didn't notice the cold beneath her, only his heat, his lips, his whispered words.

The throbbing pain of her arm brought her back to the real world. 'Ouch.'

He moved away instantly, helping her to sit up again. 'Sorry. Got carried away. I didn't think about that.'

She smiled. 'I think you were pretty well distracted.'

He grinned, a look of triumph flushing his face. 'I think you were too.'

Yes, she had been. But it came crashing back and she buried her head in her hands. 'What are we going to do?' She acknowledged she had said 'we'; she had just claimed him.

'I don't think there's too much to do, except try it and see how we go.'

He didn't seem to understand the problem. 'But you're a Verindal. I'm a Vendel … almost.'

He puffed out a laugh. 'Didn't we just go through that? Remember, things aren't what they were when our parents were our age, and certainly not our grandparents. They faced all those restrictions about no Vendel and Verindal ever having relationships and laughed.'

'Not exactly,' she countered. 'They nearly killed my father for loving my mother when she was on the throne of Verindon. And they nearly killed *her* when they discovered the truth about her parents.'

'You know, you need to forgive them for that.'

His words caught her by surprise. What did he mean? 'Who am I supposed to forgive?'

'Your parents *and* your grandparents,' he said evenly. 'I don't know what your grandmother went through when she was the overlord's consort or what made her have an affair with an agent, but neither do you. You don't know the choices or decisions or pressures she was under and why she did what she did. And even if it's true that she was a manipulative cheater, which I *really* can't imagine, given what we know of her, that's still not your mother's fault.'

This was bizarre. 'I don't blame my mother.'

'Yes, you do. You screw up your mouth a bit whenever you talk about her. You're ashamed of her.'

'I'm not!' But a bell inside her head chimed at her words. Was it possible that her lie-detecting skill reacted when *she* was lying?

He didn't raise his voice. 'Yes, you are, Missy. And she knows it. She's talked to my mother about it. I overheard them. You need to find a way to get past that. Remember, your mother's not responsible for her parentage any more than you are. She can't help what they chose to do. She can only live with their choices and try and do her best in spite of them.'

Her heart dropped into her stomach. Did she really hate her mother? Resent her for something that was beyond her control? She knew she often had problems with her, but that was because she wasn't *really* an agent, not like Father. She had never been trained properly. She had no real abilities. That's why she'd gone into diplomacy rather than on missions or training at the Academy. She had no skills or talent, except at lie detecting.

But even as she pondered this, she could feel the heat of her anger. Her body betrayed her, declaring in the tautness of her shoulders, in the scowl she could feel forming on her face. She *did* resent her mother. Not for being less of an agent than she could be. After all, Mother hadn't had the formal training Father had had. And why hadn't she? Because she'd been hidden away on Lisenus—on Earth—to hide the truth about *her parentage*.

Jolan was right. Everything she struggled with about her mother, every problem she had, every deficiency she found had sprung up because of what her mother was—a crossbreed. How many times had she been furious at her peers for branding her with the same mark? How many times had she sat simmering in silence, knowing she would show them what kind of an agent she could be in spite of her mixed blood? Ready to be the best to demonstrate that she could do it all, even with Verindal blood.

And she'd resented her mother for the same thing. Expected her to be better, to overcome, to be more than she was, so she didn't have to look at her and be ashamed.

She was a fool. She could hardly look at Jolan now she'd acknowledged it to herself—that she'd treated her mother the same way she hated being treated.

He must have seen this on her face because he reached out and stroked her arm. 'It's all right. I know you love her. I'm sure she does too. It's hard to struggle with things like that, to get past something that we find difficult to deal with in ourselves.' He raised his eyebrows. 'Wow, listen to me. When did I get so deep and serious?' He smirked at her. 'That must be your influence.'

She was relieved he was making light of it as the shame of her treatment of her mother brought her low. She gave him a watery smile. 'At least I'm good for something.'

'You're good for plenty,' he chided her. 'And one thing you're going to be especially good at is working out our next step. What is the next step, anyway?'

And just like that, he erased her guilt and moved on, rather than harping about her failings or lecturing her anymore. Not that she needed it; she felt bad enough about it herself. But there was no doubt he'd picked up on that and knew they didn't need to talk about it anymore.

Part of her didn't want to let things go so easily. It was in her to work through things until they were resolved. But she couldn't do much about her feelings for her mother while they were languishing on Darsair. And he was right—they needed to turn their attention back to what they could do to get home.

CHAPTER SIXTEEN

Misilina watched the light on the door grow dimmer. Soon it would be time to move.

She peered through the warped glass. She could see little of the road beyond. There hadn't been much sign of life since she'd been awake; maybe a few rebels shouting in the distance. Once, she'd heard the sound of a Tekkon crowd control roller. She'd thought of trying to flag it down, but she still had the nagging worry that Mandine's treachery went further than Keily alone.

There had been nothing else. No one had entered their street, no one had come to the door and there had been no attack from Keily, even though they'd been there all day. It was the most positive sign yet that they'd finally ditched their pursuer.

But that didn't help when it came to the next part of their task. Because there was only one thing left to do—get off the planet.

She wished she could believe that Tenya was still out there, alive and fighting to find them, Amatara and Dina by her side. But she was sure they would have scoured the entire city to find them, knocked on every door, made broadcasts, anything to reach them. There had been nothing. That meant there was only one conclusion she could come to. They were dead, Tenya at least. Probably the other two as well, although it was possible that Dina and Amatara were alive but were not of a high enough experience to influence crowd control's behaviour.

But even if they couldn't influence them, they knew the procedures as well as she did. It was nearly twenty Darsairian maxispans since their

142

mission had been compromised. They would definitely have been making their presence known throughout the city to try and signal them. The silence sounded their death knell louder than anything else.

Jolan was playing with the laser pistol they'd stolen. He snapped it up, flicked on its power cell, aimed and let it fall, over and over again. He'd been doing that for the past few minspans. The day before it would have annoyed her, but now she sensed all-too-clearly what it meant. 'Nervous?'

He snapped up the gun, flicked the cell, aimed and let it fall. 'What makes you think that?'

She turned and put her hand over his, stilling him. 'This will work. I've calculated every step. I know exactly where we're going and exactly how to get there. I'm pretty sure that together we can pilot the Star Runner.'

He snapped up the gun, flicked the cell, aimed and let it fall. 'I know how well you plan. But you know as well as I do that this is the step they'll anticipate.'

She scowled. Yes, it was. Keily knew she was armed. She knew she had sugar. The next step was to ensure Jolan's safety. 'But I know this place well. I've studied every part of it.'

He dropped his hand, leaning back against the wall. 'Yeah, but we don't have all the latest information, do we? What's changed out there? What have the rebels done to the city?' He rubbed his hands together, clearing them of the dust that had gathered there. 'What I wouldn't give for a comm unit. Or a wrist comm. Or anything, really.' He looked at her. 'Are you sure we shouldn't contact the Tekkon government?'

That was the dilemma. 'I worry about it. Their government has never been known for its honesty. What if they helped Mandine? What if they're waiting for us to reveal ourselves so they can hand us over to her?'

'That's possible. But even if they are, I've been thinking about it, and I'm not sure an elite of her level could have influenced them that far. I mean, what do she and her family have to offer? Her father doesn't have much by way of mines or wealth. While I think he's probably made a deal somewhere, I'm not sure it's with the government. And if it is, it may not be all of them.'

He made a lot of sense. 'Still ...'

'I'm a known figure. The crowd control forces will be likely to recognise me. I think we'd have to be extremely unlucky to run into any crowd control they might have corrupted.'

'But you don't know that for sure.'

'No. But you have contingency plans. And remember, they'll have been contacted by our people also. There's likely already a team on the way from Verindon. We've just got to reach them. And remember Ambassador Utreysin. He'll back us up. He may have already done that.'

He was painting the picture brighter than it was in her head. Even if the Tekkon government had had nothing to do with Mandine's betrayal, they were still busy dealing with the rebellion and may not care about them. Given the level of corruption in the government, money might be the only thing that swayed them and they could only offer the promise of that. They had nothing solid to hand over—no precious gems, no jewels, not even evidence of a line of credit.

But the only other thing they could do was sneak into the docking station and commandeer the Star Runner. Something that Keily would anticipate. They would be walking straight into her arms.

They'd discussed this earlier and Jolan still couldn't let it go. 'You know they'll be there waiting for us. But if we go to the government, we could circumvent that. I'm still the son of the overlord. If we promise them riches, we're more likely to deliver than Mandine. That's got to stand for something.'

That was true, but it still didn't mean she wanted to march out onto the street and straight up to the nearest crowd control unit.

'You know what we could do,' she said. 'Commandeer another ship. There are over three hundred bays in that station. We don't have to go anywhere near the Star Runner. A small ship is all we need and will probably be easier for us to pilot.' The roof of each landing bay opened automatically as each individual ship began its launch procedure and Darsair had no landing control beam or anything that could stop them once they'd cleared the station. They could make a clean getaway.

It was disappointing to think they'd have to effectively steal a ship, but she was sure Overlord Ardon would either send the ship back or recompensate the owner for it.

'Also, we can make use of the sewer lines,' she said, thinking aloud.

He raised his eyebrows. 'Are you telling me they still have sewers here? No automatic waste disposal stations?'

'No. And they go right up to the docking station.' And since the station was at the better end of town, the plans she'd seen were likely to be more up to date.

He gagged. 'I don't like the thought of that, but I guess … How long will it take us to get to an entry point?'

'There's one several streets away. Not too close, unfortunately, in this part of the city. We'll have to walk a bit to get there.'

The light dulled and waned and the street globes began to glow. It was time to move. She took his hand. But he snatched her into his arms and pressed his lips to hers, drawing her closer and wrapping her arms around his neck. He held her for a few minspans, his mouth on hers, his hands in her hair, until she pulled away. 'We need to go.'

He chuckled guiltily. 'Sorry. I just needed a bit of courage.'

'Really?' He was that worried? What he'd said didn't sound completely true but she wasn't sure it was a lie either.

He smirked. 'Nah, I just thought it would be fun.'

That was only *mostly* true. 'Let's go.'

They pulled aside the door, Misilina wincing as the sound cracked in the gloom of twilight. They looked out. There was no one in sight. She hefted her firearm. 'Come on.'

She ignored the pain in her arm, which gave a throb as they left the safety of their hideout. She wished they could stay there. She wished she was able to receive a message from Tenya or from the Star Runner that would be on its way, loaded with agents. Maybe even her father, coming to their rescue. While he was right that the Verindonian ambassador was still likely alive and well—he hadn't attended the mine visit—one word kept buzzing in her mind. Corruption. How far did it extend? She would much rather put her hope in the Star Runners that were likely to land soon.

She was sure of one thing, however—they hadn't arrived yet. Even if she no longer had a comm unit, agents would have swarmed the streets searching for them. That meant that the Darsairian leadership was delaying them. Why, she wasn't sure. Had they been paid off by Mandine? Surely she didn't have enough clout to influence the government of the entire planet. Tekkon's maybe, but the governing body of all Darsair?

They stepped out into the street. It was just as quiet and deserted as it had been when they'd entered. Misilina examined the dust that caked the pavement and the road. There were no signs of steps other than their own. Good.

She slowed her pace as they approached the corner of the street. There were faint sounds to their right—muffled shouting, probably some distance away, and the faint sound of rollers. It was likely crowd control trying to quell the riot.

It was best they stayed away from the crowds if they could. They could easily be mistaken for miners, especially since they were still wearing their mining clothes. They didn't want to attract attention from the rioters or crowd control.

She clutched the firearm tighter. The knife they'd taken from the Darsairian was hidden in her pant leg; she'd used a strip from Jolan's shirt to strap it there. Fortunately, he had stripped it from the bottom, so the shirt was still good enough to wear, if a little short on him. She could see the base of his spine peeking out as he walked past ... that was a distraction she didn't need.

Instead, she glanced down at the four sugar canisters she'd managed to attach to a belt made from a plastic strip she'd found buried under some dust in their temporary home. It wasn't as sturdy as the belt of her jumpsuit, but it would have to do. They would keep her fighting.

She turned left, Jolan beside her. 'Be careful with that laser.' He had the small firearm.

'I'm not entirely incapable when it comes to weapons, you know,' he replied, an edge to his voice.

As they continued, they passed a number of the city's holo displays; a sure sign they were heading back towards the higher end of town. Misilina stopped short as the image of the Tekkon governor appeared. She tried not to stare at it, pulling Jolan to the side, even though the street was deserted.

'Citizens of Tekkon,' he said, speaking in Darsairian, 'we appreciate the effort of all of you who have joined us in battling the rebellious element of the city. We now seek your help in discovering the location of our Verindonian visitors, who have gone missing. Please aid us in ascertaining if any of them are alive and especially if they are injured or in your care.'

Images of Jolan and Mandine flashed on the holo. 'If we are to retain the goodwill of our Verindonian neighbours, it's imperative we do our best to locate them. We would be grateful for your assistance. To confirm our plea, here is the Verindonian ambassador.'

His image was replaced by Ambassador Utreysin, with a sagging face and heavy eyes. 'I would like to reiterate what your governor has said.' He also spoke in Darsarian. 'Please, if you could help us locate the members of our high family, we would be forever grateful. Please offer your assistance if you can. Our people are desperate for news of their whereabouts.'

The holo dissolved back into the images of Jolan and Mandine. Misilina's heart sank. It was the most confirmation she'd had yet that Tenya and the others were dead. There had been no mention of looking for anyone other than Jolan and Mandine. And she was sure Tenya would have insisted on being featured in any communications they attempted.

She looked at Jolan. It wasn't immediately obvious who he was given the clothes he was wearing and the smudges on his face, and she was more than happy with that. In spite of this appeal, she still wasn't sure she wanted to trust the government of Tekkon, but it was clear that Jolan did.

'Come on,' he said in a low voice as they began walking again. 'You've got to admit that was a pretty good sign. And you didn't detect any lies, did you?'

'You know we can't pick up lies from recorded messages.'

But it was difficult to argue with him. If they could get the government's help, they would be instantly safe and all officials were likely to believe Jolan over Mandine. The holo implied that they didn't know where either of the elites was, so that meant that Mandine might still be working with Keily and no one else.

But maybe it didn't. Maybe it was a trap. However, the desire to make Jolan safe as quickly as possible began to take over. Agency protocols dictated that the subject of the mission should be protected above all else, and this offered a way to make him safe quickly. She needed to at least try it out.

'All right. We'll give it a shot.' She had to get as close as she could to Tekkon government headquarters in the hope of finding a crowd control force that would help them. At least now she knew they might be actively looking for them. She wasn't sure if that was a good thing or a bad thing.

The next street was a little lighter and she could see some people moving about at the other end. The people ahead of them didn't seem to be rioting, although she could see evidence of where the rioting had been. From her knowledge, this was normally a fashionable end of town that had an active nightlife, but the Darsairians she saw at the other end of the street didn't look like that type. As they got closer, she realised they were doing trade, much the same as the trader they'd stolen their weapons from—probably low-grade gems, cheap stimulants, perhaps even their bodies. Maybe they'd moved in temporarily to take advantage of the quiet that the riots had enforced.

At least they were the kind of people who would go about their business and be unlikely to approach them. She walked confidently past them, holding her head high. They turned and glanced at the two of them, and she saw one or two lingering glances. She wondered if they'd seen the holo. But they simply watched and went back to their business. Hopefully, Jolan's miner's garb was a convincing disguise.

At the end of the street, there were more signs of earlier rioting—some places of business and even a public viewing station had been torn to pieces and torched. Debris littered the ground and the technical components leaked choking spires of smoke. They stepped around it and moved on. Misilina estimated that the rioting there had taken place a few maxispans ago, while it had still been light. The instigators had probably been so drunk on their success, and maybe on other things, that they had thrown caution to the wind.

She could sense Jolan's presence just behind her. 'Still know where you are?' he asked.

'We'll get there.'

Most streets were the same—a few night workers, little else. Occasionally in the distance there were the faint sounds of rebellion, almost immediately followed by the whine of crowd control alerts.

They were two streets away from the Tekkon government district when she looked around the corner and saw what she had both sought and dreaded—crowd control at a border examining a group of locals. The ten people in their midst had their heads down and they were crouched together, the force of five keeping their long-barrelled weapons trained on them.

This is it. 'Come on.' She would have to be careful. Would her lie-detecting ability sound off if any of the crowd control lied to her? She knew that Darsairian voices took a low tone when they were lying, so she would have to listen for that as well.

They turned the corner, their presence immediately noted by the crowd control force, one pointing. 'Look, two more.'

Misilina put her weapon in her belt and raised her hands, nodding at Jolan to do the same. 'We're no danger to you,' she said in Darsairian.

'We're two of the Verindonians your government is looking for.'

Two of the crowd control approached, their weapons trained on them, their dark uniforms making it difficult to distinguish them from the night. Both had helmets that shielded their faces. Misilina tried not to panic when they took their firearms. Fortunately, they didn't frisk her and find the knife strapped to her leg.

Jolan squared his shoulders, a regal look on his face. 'Your government is concerned about our safety and you disarm us?'

She wished she could see their faces so she could read them. She tried to assess their voices instead. 'You're the Verindonian royal, Jolan?' their leader said, holding a holo image of him up to her visor.

'That's correct.'

The dark helmet turned to her. 'And this is?'

'One of my trusted agents who has done her best to keep me safe. I demand that we be taken immediately to Ambassador Utreysin's quarters. I'm sure he's waiting for us there.'

The faceless visor gazed at her for a moment longer before turning back to Jolan. 'Of course, leader.'

Lie. Misilina made sure there was no pause in her step as she moved between the woman and Jolan, making it appear they were following her back to the rest of the force. She was in the safety zone in the next microspan, snatched the leader's weapon and turned it on them, spraying them with fire.

Everyone dived for cover. She ran backwards, Jolan going forwards, heading back the way they'd come, continuing to fire on crowd control. Fortunately, they didn't start returning fire until they'd reached the end of the street. Once around the corner, Misilina turned and started running beside Jolan.

'They were lying?' he said.

'Clearly. I'm sorry, we can't trust them.' Even if not all the crowd control forces were corrupted, they couldn't risk it. How would they know whether they were trustworthy or not until it was too late?

'I can't believe Mandine could have ...' Jolan growled. 'Never mind. When we catch up with her, I'll kill her myself.' She wondered if he meant it. He certainly had reason to, but Misilina wasn't so sure. However angry he was, she couldn't imagine him doing something like that. Killing her in a fight was more likely. And he could probably beat Mandine.

Keily was going to be the big problem. It would be up to Misilina to take her down. And while Keily didn't seem that great at hitting her target on the first shot, she had better aim the longer she fired. Maybe it took her a while to warm up. So if Misilina did face Keily, she needed to take her down as quickly as possible. And if Jolan couldn't defeat Mandine, she would have to tackle both of them.

At least Keily hadn't been waiting out there for them, something that worried her. She looked up at the walls around them as they continued running, terrified that shots would rain down on them. She kept her senses focused as widely as she could, hoping she could anticipate any threat to Jolan before it came.

It surprised her that Keily wasn't there, but it was at least more evidence that she could no longer track them. That was about the only point they had against her. But Misilina was sure that, even now, intel about what had happened was being communicated to Keily and Mandine—intel the assassin could use against them.

A curl of fear wound its way through Misilina's stomach. What if she couldn't do this? She had only just graduated. Keily had killed all Jolan's squad and probably the rest of hers as well, all of whom had more experience than her. Decades, in some cases. Was there any hope she could win?

She knew she couldn't start thinking like that. If she did, she'd hand victory to Keily. She had to concentrate on her mission—getting Jolan home. She *would* succeed.

Even if it cost her own life.

And it helped that she'd already planned the next step. She'd known exactly where to go as soon as they'd begun their retreat. Jolan knew it too, that's why he'd asked no questions.

Misilina darted down a side street, checking her senses to ensure that Jolan was still with her, then made three more quick turns left, then right, then right, all the time heading for the closest conduit that led to their new destination. Back to the original plan—take the sewers to the docking station.

Finally, the entry was in front of them. She stopped at the large circular dent in the roadway and began to turn it. It was hard work, given that she had to stretch her arms out fully to hold the catches at its end. This was normally a two-person job.

Jolan realised that instantly. 'Here, you turn that side, I'll turn this one.' She nodded, feeling the safety zone begin to fade away. They needed to get under cover before it did. She couldn't risk having to go back into the zone immediately and using another can of sugar.

After a few more arm-wrenching turns, Misilina felt the cover loosen. Soon it began to wind up in front of them, revealing a black and fetid hole. She could see a grime-coated metal rung through the dim light from the street globes—the first step on the ladder down to the sewers.

To his credit, Jolan didn't complain or even comment on the smell. He held his nose, though, as he turned around to start his descent. He looked up at her as he disappeared into the blackness. 'I hope this works.'

'It will.' It had to. There was nothing else they could do. She climbed onto the ladder, reaching for the relocking mechanism on the underside of the hole cover. She stepped down a few rungs, pulling the cover shut behind her, winding it shut again. It was a lot easier to do it on this side, probably because it had to be to release any trapped workers. After all, only one of them could be on the ladder at once.

It ground shut again, just as the safety zone left her completely. She took a deep breath to still her racing heart and reached for a can of sugar.

Three cans left.

CHAPTER SEVENTEEN

Misilina listened at the top of the ladder for a few minspans and heard sounds of a pursuit, but they clattered over the top of the conduit without noticing anything amiss. Good.

She turned her attention to the sounds below her. She could hear ragged sounds from Jolan as he tried to breathe through his mouth and the trickle of sewage as it flowed through the channels beneath them. The smell became powerfully obvious in the next moment, turning her stomach. It was a good thing they hadn't had anything to eat since the previous night, as it would have decorated the wall.

She heard a slight splash. It sounded like Jolan had reached the bottom of the ladder. She'd told him to wait there for her, and he did, thankfully. Once she'd joined him, she knew why—the tunnel they were standing in extended to the left and right, both ways leading into impenetrable darkness.

'What do we do now? I guess you know the way,' Jolan said.

She shrugged. 'More or less.'

She couldn't see his face but could hear the shock in his voice. 'More or less? Missy, are you telling me you led us down here and you don't know where we're going?'

She hoped so. The plans of this section had *seemed* up to date, but what if they weren't? And it hadn't occurred to her to think about how dark they would be. As she peered around, she tried to get some sense of the right way. She was sure it was left but being underground in total darkness was disorientating.

'Missy? Which way do we go?'

'I *think* to the left.'

She heard him suck in a breath. Had he realised she was clueless? Perhaps he did because his response was calmer than she would have thought. 'Okay, we go left. Any idea what to do about the light ... or lack of it?'

Time to admit her failing. 'I haven't got a clue.'

If the silence was anything to go by, he hadn't expected that. But again, there was no complaint. 'At least you're still armed.'

'Yes.' She wasn't sure the model of gun she'd swiped from crowd control, but there was no doubt it was better than her last one.

'Don't Darsairian Crowd Control usually have the F–120Z as their go-to weapon?'

'I believe so.' She hadn't given it a lot of thought. To her surprise, she felt him fumble for it in her hand, taking the weapon from her. 'What are you doing?'

'You know a lot of things about a lot of things, darling, but I know my weapons.' The gun let out a trill, which was accompanied by a small but intense light that pierced a hole in the darkness. The tunnel around them took on an icy blue hue as her eyes grew used to the strange glow from the gun.

She looked up into Jolan's face. His smirk was tinged with blue but still triumphant. 'See? I have my uses.'

That look on his face would have annoyed her to death before they'd arrived on this planet. Now, she felt the urge to kiss him and saw no reason to suppress it. She pressed her lips to his, feeling his victorious smile. He tried to hand the gun back to her, but she pushed it into his hands, taking out her knife. 'You keep that and light the way.'

He grinned. 'You're going to defend us with just the knife?'

Was that a challenge? 'Don't you think I can?'

His smile grew wider. 'I think you can do anything you want to.'

'Fine, then you lead the way.' She wasn't sure if it was a good

154

idea for him to go first, but she hoped the light would give them ample warning of an approaching enemy. And behind them was only darkness. If Jolan knew how the gun worked, it stood to reason that he could at least get off a warning shot if something came their way. He might not be so lucky with an attack from behind. And she'd done sufficient training with real blades, virtual ones, electro-blades, fire-shock blades ... Yes, it was better she watched their backs.

'But now, it's up to you,' he said. 'Which way do we go?'

'Left.' She tried to picture the map of the sewers in her mind, laid out beneath the streets. She had noted several entry points for them and the one they'd used was about a distance from the docking station, taking into account the curves of the streets. The tunnels' layout was a little different again, so it would take a bit of navigating for her to get it right if every tunnel was still the same as it was in the plans. And she couldn't afford an error. One mistake could force them back to the streets.

So they began their trudge through the stinking sewers, Misilina trying to ignore the mud—maybe something worse than mud—that she could feel coating her shoes. She tried to discreetly shake off the pieces of caked-on filth and knew Jolan was doing the same thing.

Fortunately, Misilina had something to distract her attention, being focused on which way to go. It meant that she only noticed the putrid odour every second breath. And they couldn't go quickly. She measured every step, paused at every junction, considering carefully which one to take.

Jolan waited patiently while she decided on the way forward for them, always maintaining silence when she was standing at a fork, looking back and forth, remembering ... Once she'd started up again, he would occasionally make conversation.

He looked at the cans strapped to her belt. 'You've still got three?'

'Yes.'

'We'll need those where we're heading.'

It was good he understood that. It was also good he didn't realise she'd probably need about ten of them to beat Keily unless she took the sniper out with her first shot.

They continued sloshing through the muck, the sound of trickling water their constant companion. That and a regular drip … drip … *drip*! Occasional plunks and plops filled her mind with images of what was joining them in the sewers. It was difficult to keep her stomach from churning.

As they entered a crossway for several different tunnels, Misilina froze. There was a new sound. This was more like a sliding, slithering. Then a shuffle.

Was someone or something down there with them?

Jolan stopped too, so it wasn't her imagination. She gritted her teeth. Did she zone? It would use up a valuable sugar canister and she couldn't be sure—

'Well, what do we have here?'

Jolan shone their light on the man who approached them. He was short and dragged one leg along. That at least identified the source of the sliding sound. He gave a gap-toothed grin, his scruffy miner's haircut sticking out in all directions. His clothes were, however, relatively new and looked tailored. Did he have access to a virtual clothes program or did he have connections?

His words alerted Misilina to the fact that he was not alone. A filthy woman sidled up on their right. She was younger than the man but just as well dressed even though her shirt was splattered with mud and the cuffs of her finely-cut coat looked a little worn.

Not virtual clothes, then.

The most disturbing thing was whoever was coming up behind them. Misilina didn't turn to look; she let her ears see for her. He sounded large and she didn't think he was Darsairian. But something was familiar about the sense of him, the size, the feel she got from him.

He was a Randoid. It stood to reason that there might be some on Darsair. It was likely they used Randoids for heavy lifting in the mines as their arms had three times the strength of most humanoid species. And the only way to kill one, as she knew well, was a shot directly into their ear flap.

She was definitely going to have to use some precious sugar to get out of this. And she couldn't escape the thrill of nerves that went through her as she remembered what had happened the last time she'd fought a Randoid, and that one had only been virtual.

Making sure she was tuned to his movements, she kept a periphery eye on the woman and directed her gaze at the man. He didn't seem troubled and cast a greedy look over their gun. 'You two must know how to handle yourselves if you took that from crowd control.'

Jolan shrugged and kept his eyes forward, although a twitch in his neck told Misilina he had some idea of the attack waiting behind them. 'Maybe the person we stole it from did.'

He was trying to lull them into a false sense of security. Given the confidence exuding from the male, she didn't think that was necessary. 'Elal,' he said to the woman, 'you need a new gun, don't you?'

Elal grabbed the end of a long red braid of hair and flicked it. It took Misilina a moment to realise that it wasn't her hair. Her head was shaved. The braid hung from a cord at her neck, with several more braids of different colours on her belt.

Elal passed her eyes over Misilina's brunette braid. 'A new gun … amongst other things, hey, Varl?'

Misilina felt Jolan tense beside her, especially as the Randoid let out an echoing guffaw. However, her companion smiled. 'We're always in the market for a good trade.' She could see what he was angling for. He was hoping that perhaps the gun, or even Misilina's braid, might be enough to get them to leave them in peace. But that was their only real weapon and she would die rather than give it up. And she wasn't about to do that.

The safety zone was her only hope. She could never defeat a Randoid without it. And he was only one of them. This was so much worse than her training simulations!

And a Randoid needed to be killed with a shot in their ear canal. A *shot*. Yes, she could snatch the gun from Jolan easily enough, but he had two Darsairians to face.

Could she kill the Randoid with a knife? Official data said no, it wouldn't penetrate deep enough, but it could incapacitate him briefly, perhaps giving her enough time to deal with Elal and Varl before returning for the killing blow.

Varl took a step forward the moment the Randoid did. Misilina zoned instantly, leaping up to the ceiling of the tunnel and using her enhanced abilities to run along it until she was behind her target. As she passed his head, she reached down and took it in her hands. She tried to manoeuvre her knife over his ear flap, but her angle wasn't perfect and he bucked under her grip, his long arms wrapping around her. She dropped down onto the floor of the tunnel, dragging him with her.

She hoped fervently that Jolan's training would help him hold the other two off, that any weapons they had were inferior, anything that would help him survive, as she tightened her hold on the Randoid's head. He shook it, flinging her about the tunnel, one foot connecting with the wall. She was glad he didn't know about her still aching arm. It throbbed with every movement, but thankfully, the safety zone helped her ignore the pain.

He reached up to try and dislodge her, digging his fingers into her skin. She knew she had to incapacitate him while she still had hold of him, so dragged his head down into the mud at their feet, trying to position her knife at the right angle. But he was wise to her plan and reached up, grabbing her head and slamming it into the sludge at her feet. She landed face-up, still grasping his head, trying to line up her knife. But he had the upper hand now and a sneer passed over his face as he gripped her.

She wouldn't lose to a Randoid again. She pinned herself to the floor of the tunnel and using all her enhanced strength, put her feet to his chest, striking him as hard as she could. He stumbled backwards and she leapt on him, using the safety zone to line up his ear canal, her knife at the ready.

'Missy!'

She dropped the knife, the safety zone alerting her before the laser landed in her hand. She slammed it against the Randoid's head, using the barrel to slip under the ear flap, giving him a full blast. She watched his eyes flash with flame before the colour faded, leaving only a bemused look on his misshapen face.

She vaulted around, seeking her new enemies, only to see two bodies lying in the sewage, Jolan standing over them. She looked at him, impressed. 'You did that on your own?'

He looked around in the blaster light, finding the knife and wiping the gunk off it. 'It wasn't that hard. They only had knives.'

'They probably thought the Randoid would take care of both of us without a problem.' She examined the neat blast points in Varl's head and Elal's chest. Jolan was a better shot than she'd thought. That was good. Maybe he *could* take on Mandine by himself. But she doubted he would be able to kill her, regardless of what she'd done to him. Hopefully, he could incapacitate her enough that he could make his escape, even if he needed to pilot a ship alone. But she wasn't going to tell him that. She was sure any suggestion that she give her life so he could get away would be met with vehement resistance. And they had to reach the docking station first.

Misilina looked around, trying to orientate herself in the tunnels again. It was difficult given that four tunnels met at that junction—all dark and gloomy, all covered in identical slime with identical drips and plinks. Which way was the right one?

Something caught her eye—a dark mass leaning against the side of the tunnel where Varl had been standing. Could it be another assailant? She indicated to Jolan to get behind her and began creeping forward. Surely there wouldn't be another one. She was down to two cans of sugar.

Jolan sloshed along. She flinched at every noise he made, but she wasn't much quieter. That was probably how Varl and his gang had found them. Or perhaps they'd unwittingly come too close to something a bit more precious. It soon became clear that the dark obtrusion was not another being. Misilina lifted a sack to reveal what horde the gang had been protecting.

There were several large packets of uncut mining gems, a few bags with astralin, a recreational drug, but what delighted her was the long-barrelled high-range laser rifle.

Jolan raised his eyebrows as he looked over their booty. 'Hm. Looks like they were well-resourced.'

'Lucky for us.' Misilina picked up the rifle and looked through the sights, checking the energy cell. It wasn't full, but more than half the cell was charged. It should be enough. If she couldn't take out Keily quickly, she would have more to worry about than a slight cell drain.

She examined the stash more carefully. 'No sugar.'

'You could try the astralin,' Jolan said, a smile in his voice.

She gave him a look even though she could tell he was only joking.

'What?' he said. 'It could kick you back into the safety zone. I mean, sure, you'd be a little unsteady on your feet ...'

'That would *really* help in beating Keily.'

'Okay, so it's not the best idea I've ever had.' He seemed light-hearted, perhaps because their journey was nearing its end. 'Do you think we need their knives as well?'

She glanced at him. 'How good are you at fighting with knives?'

He wrinkled his nose. 'Not that great.'

'Then just the one I got from the gem seller will do.'

'But that rifle should help a lot, right?'

He was right. It gave them an edge. It might be just enough to get them through. 'And do you know the best thing about it?'

'What?'

'That Keily and Mandine don't know we have it.' So far Keily had been one step ahead of them, but this time, she would have no idea what they were bringing into battle against her. So they stood a chance, a better one than she had thought a maxispan ago. Would it be enough?

CHAPTER EIGHTEEN

Misilina still had to work out which way they should go. It took some time for her to reorientate herself, going back to the crossway and looking at where the bodies of Varl, Elal and the Randoid lay, and remembering which way she'd been heading. Looking over it again gave her more confidence. She could see the way they'd come. She'd been sure they'd needed to veer left and there was only one tunnel that took them in that direction.

She carried the rifle and the knife she'd got from the gem dealer and left the crowd control laser with Jolan. He'd already proven he was proficient with it. She would have loved a smaller firearm as well, in case it came to close fighting with Keily, but figured she'd have to rely on the knife for that. And given that the lady-in-waiting seemed to be a sniper first and foremost, Misilina might not get near enough for close-range anything.

She tried to put that thought out of her mind, instead running through as many scenarios as she could to plan for every possible outcome. It was hard when so many of them ended in at least her death, but most allowed Jolan time to escape. She was determined that if Keily took her down, she would take the sniper with her.

Jolan didn't say much. Whenever she caught a glimpse of his face in the blaster's dull blue light, he still seemed confident. He wasn't brilliant at hiding his feelings, so she hoped he wasn't dwelling on what could go wrong, and there was plenty.

Eventually, Misilina clenched the rifle tighter and slowed. 'We're getting close to our destination. Pretty soon there'll be another ladder, which we'll take back to the surface. If I've got everything right, we should be about a span from the docking station.'

Jolan nodded. 'How do we get in?'

'There are three different entryways. There's a service entrance not far from where we'll return to the street. It's the most straightforward way in. There may be personnel there, although I'm assuming there'll be less traffic than usual at the docking station owing to the riots. I could be wrong about that, of course. Not that it makes much of a difference, as there are still likely to be workers there, so we shouldn't use that way if we don't have to.

'The way we're most likely to use will be an air vent that leads to the first landing bay. It's on the second level, so we'd have to go up the side of the building to get in.'

'How do we do that?'

'It's not hard; numerous worker lifters go up there. As far as I know, they don't have any alarms or triggers and they're all worker-operated.

'The third way is the best, but it's a little trickier. It's a conveyor belt that leads into the station from the supply depot. The trouble with that is there are bound to be workers resupplying all the bays, even if they're not all that active at the moment. But it's the best because we could make it a long way into the station.'

'Do you remember which landing bay the Star Runner is in?'

'Number ten.' Or as near to it as Darsairian numerals got. 'So we don't want to be near that. We'll try and get to another section and see what we can locate.'

'But getting in that way is the hard part,' he said.

'It'll depend on whether there's a crate we can commandeer.' She looked up, seeing the bottom rung of the ladder she had expected to find. Wrapping her hands around it, she looked at the dilapidated tunnel with its stinking fetid scummy water. It suddenly felt like the safest option.

But they couldn't stay down there forever. Pulling herself hand over hand, she headed back to street level, Jolan right behind her.

With a creak, the cover opened, although she made sure only a little at first. She breathed a sigh of relief when she realised she was exactly where she was supposed to be. She listened carefully. There was the sound of workers, but they weren't too near.

She could only see part of the streetscape, as this cover was hinged, so blocked her view of the other side. It should be nothing more than the bottom pylon holding up the docking station's rail link. While she knew some local vagrants might have taken up residence there, it was unlikely there would be anyone else ... usually, anyway.

There was no help for it—she had to take the risk. She pushed the cover open and climbed out, immediately bringing her weapon to bear as she scanned the street. There were a couple of grimy figures sleeping underneath a pylon, but they barely stirred as she crept closer to check that they were no threat. The rest of the street was silent, bathed in the light from Tekkon's street globes.

She glanced back at the conduit where Jolan peered out, nodding at him. He quickly climbed through, closing it behind him, not bothering to seal it. It was possible they might need to use it again, although that would be the worst-case scenario.

Well, not quite. The worst-case scenario would mean they were both dead.

He joined her, squinting up and down the street, then looked back at her. She'd cautioned him about speaking unless he had to.

Misilina ducked to the other side of the pylons that lined the street at regular intervals all the way to the docking station. They weren't perfect cover, but the girders that attached to the rail above were tall, wide and heavy, and would make it difficult for someone to get a decent shot.

Would it stop Keily? Probably not, but she would hopefully miss her first shot, as usual, alerting them to her presence. And she wouldn't know for sure which way they'd come from, so why wait out there when she could wait for them inside? They had to go into the docking station; it was the only option left.

Still, it was better to be safe than sorry, as her mother often said. So they darted in and out of the pylons, holding their weapons high. Misilina dissected every sound, ready for any assailant, any threat.

As they crept closer to the station, she put out a hand to slow him. The voices were clearer and she could see workers unloading a transit wagon on the rail above them. They brought the merchandise down to street-level via the lifters, although some of it was taken in through another entry up near the rail. There were about ten workers that she could see; it would be difficult to get past them to enter at all.

'Look,' Jolan hissed.

She saw what he was pointing at. The workers had stacked several large crates at the bottom of the lifter, each one being moved by a small mover to a nearby chute.

'Is that what you meant?'

She wasn't sure. There could have been another loading chute close by or more further on. However, from what she could remember, there was only one this close and it led to a conveyer belt that travelled around the whole station. 'Let's go.'

One of the crates had reached the ground but there were no workers close to it. She sprinted towards it, Jolan on her heels, and kept the crate between them and the workers.

She ran her hands along its hard metal surface. It was an old model, not like the ones they used on Verindon, which would have opened at a beep from her comm unit, if she'd had one. She ran her hands over the corners, hoping there was some kind of mechanism that triggered the opening, something manual—no tech.

'Here.' Jolan's hands moved over hers and pulled back a metal plate. Inside was a basic catch mechanism.

There was enough noise around them to cover the sound of the crate's side squeaking open. Inside, there were several smaller metal boxes, some cables and globe fixtures. Misilina grabbed the lightweight fixtures and shoved them to the side. Fortunately, the crate wasn't full, leaving enough room for them, although it was a squeeze—she had to sit on top of the metal boxes and Jolan stuffed himself in amongst the cables. Jolan pulled the door closed behind them, keeping his fingers in the gap. Misilina prayed that the workers wouldn't notice. She also hoped the crate wouldn't slam shut and take off his fingers.

She listened to her heart beating as they sat in silence and darkness, hearing the sound of the team on duty coming closer. As their voices sounded not far away, Jolan dropped his mouth close to her ear. 'Did you hear that?' he whispered.

She put her hand over his mouth. This was not the time to speak.

There was no indication that the workers checked the crate for anything and in a few minspans, she felt the floor sway as they were lifted into the air. She joined Jolan in holding the door shut; the last thing they needed was for the contents to fall out and rain down on the surprised workers below. No doubt it would be a shock to see a Verindal royal and a Vendel agent lying amongst shattered globes and fractured electrical parts. The frequent jolting smashed the door against her fingers and she gritted her teeth to stop hissing from the pain.

Before they got too much further, Jolan picked up a cable from behind him. He threaded part of it through the door's catch, tying the other end to his hand, using it to hold the door shut without letting it lock.

A few minspans later, a huge jolt made Jolan's head collide with the ceiling. He shoved his fist in his mouth to keep silent. There was little she could do other than put a hand on his arm to reassure him. There was another, smaller jolt and the crate began moving again. She surmised that they were on the conveyor belt, which hopefully meant they were inside the station. She could have danced with glee. Keily was bound to be there somewhere, but how could she possibly tell where they were? Perhaps she could scan the crates for lifeforms, but would she bother to do that? Not here, with so many workers around. Maybe later. Maybe not at all, as they couldn't stay in there forever anyway.

But hopefully, she'd be waiting at the Star Runner and they could find another ride before she even realised they were there.

'How do we know when to get out?' Jolan asked, keeping his voice low, although still loud enough to be heard over the rumbling of the conveyor.

'We don't. We'll have to guess.' The only thing that really mattered was that it wasn't near the Star Runner.

'You know, when we first got into the crate, I thought I'd heard something.'

That's right. He'd mentioned it just as the workers had reached them. 'What was it?'

'An engine.'

Was that all? 'There were a lot of engines going, Jolan.'

'No, it was a ship. And I'm sure it was a Star Runner. At least one.'

'Are you sure?' She couldn't remember hearing anything, but she hadn't trained herself to recognise the nuances of individual engines. She made a mental note to add that to her list of skills ... if she survived.

'I'm positive. So help could have arrived.'

He could be right. He could also have misheard. But it meant that not only might there be reinforcements from Verindon, they might be in this very building. If that was true, Keily had no chance.

But even if their people were there, there were over three hundred bays in this station. The Star Runner might have landed in bay seven while the two of them searched for a ship in bay one hundred and ninety-six.

She would keep an eye out for any sign of a Verindonian but couldn't rely on it. She had to stick to her original plan.

It was impossible to know the right time to leave the crate. She wracked her brains for any understanding of which way they were going and how far into the station they might be. Did she dare take a peek?

She asked Jolan to loosen the cable slightly and the door swayed open a little. They were jolting along a conveyor belt behind the bays on the ground level. As they moved along, she could see various metal stairs and lifters linking this, the maintenance area, to the different floors. She could see some crates being shunted into lifters and rising to other levels, but they continued trundling along on ground level.

She snapped the door shut as the crate gave an almighty thud. A moment later, she felt them rising again. They must have been shunted off to a higher level. She would have to wait until they levelled off again before they could risk getting out. The longer they rose, the more nervous she became, although it meant they were moving deeper into the station. She tried to focus on the positives.

Finally, their crate shuddered and levelled out. She dared another peek as they passed a stained metal wall with a large symbol printed on it. She had studied Darsairian numerals. It was the equivalent of the number one hundred and sixty-seven. So they were passing bay one hundred and sixty-seven, moving onto bay one hundred and sixty-eight.

She closed the door and waited, deciding to get out at bay one hundred and eighty-two.

She didn't want to open the door too much but needed to know how long it took to pass each bay. So, a few minspans later, she whispered to Jolan and he released the cable again.

Number one hundred and seventy-four.

She calculated the approximate time it would take them to get to one hundred and eighty-two providing their pace remained steady. Then all that was left to do was wait. That wasn't easy either—she kept second-guessing everything. Did she get out earlier? Could Keily possibly find them?

Keily was clearly well-resourced. No matter the randomness of their decision, Misilina knew she would probably find them quickly. Never assume, her father had said. She couldn't rely on the sniper staying patiently at the Star Runner, waiting for them. She would have to realise they might not take the bait.

Finally, the moment arrived. 'Get ready to loosen the cable. We're getting out. As soon as you get out the door, jump off the conveyor belt and head straight for the wall with the symbol on it. There'll be a maintenance door there that leads through to the bay. We'll have to check each one individually to see if we can find a useful ship. If anyone sees us, follow my lead.' She would have to decide if they lied their way out of things or if she had to eliminate whoever found them. She didn't like doing that to someone who was just doing their job, but they couldn't risk discovery.

She prodded Jolan's shoulder and he let go of the cable, the side of the crate swinging open. She leapt down, hefting her firearm, ready to use it if shots began to rain on them. Jolan was beside her, his firearm brought to bear as well.

There were no shots and no people, just an endless parade of trundling crates. That was something, at least. Everywhere around them was dimly lit. She had no idea if this was because it was evening or simply because they liked to keep their employees in the dark. And while it was an asset when it came to concealing them from the workers, it wouldn't make a difference to Keily and her sniper rifle.

She triggered the release on the door of bay one hundred and eighty-two, which didn't appear to have a lock (presumably because entryways in this area were normally used only by employees) and crept inside. The lighting was even lower in what she discovered was an empty bay. Damn. She'd been hoping for a quick solution and a speedy departure. Now they'd have to try the next bay. And the longer they searched … 'Stay alert. We could find trouble at any time.'

'You won't go into the safety zone?'

She looked at the two cans still hanging from her belt. 'Not unless I have to.' She needed to make sure she had as much time as possible at her strongest when facing Keily. It would be handy to use her heightened senses to tell if an attack was coming, but she just had to hope that, given how many gangways, loose cables, bollards and barriers were around, there would be sufficient cover for Keily to miss her first shot and alert them to her presence.

She hurried back out, moving as quietly as she could, Jolan

copying her every move. She raced to door one hundred and eighty-three, triggered its door and looked inside.

A Bordaran crater ship. It was so huge it barely fit inside the bay. Its wing flaps were down, making it look like a giant folded box.

Jolan's shoulders slumped. 'No good. It needs a crew complement of fifteen just to start the engines.'

'And it would take the rest of the night before it had warmed up enough to make it past grav-range.' They needed to try the next bay.

They slipped out the door and moved on to bay one hundred and eighty-four. Misilina looked around carefully. There still weren't any workers around. She dragged Jolan behind some stacked crates just in case they needed cover. It was weird how quiet everything was. Given how many boxes were being transported around the bay, she would have expected at least some people around.

That thought left her cold. Yes, there should be more people around. There was only one reason why there wouldn't be. She lifted her rifle over the top of the nearest lifter and sprayed the area with fire, Jolan gaping at her in shock.

A zing and a flash exploded on a girder near her in return, revealing exactly what she'd expected. The workers weren't there because Keily had gotten rid of them somehow. How she'd discovered them so quickly Misilina didn't know, but she had. And she'd nearly been ready to make her move.

Misilina readied her weapon with a smile and put her mouth to Jolan's ear. 'I'll go into the safety zone. That should tell me exactly where she is. I'll keep her pinned down with fire while you continue checking bays. Try and find a ship that we can fly.' She didn't say 'that you can fly alone', although she wanted to. She'd just have to hope he had the sense to leave without her.

But Jolan had something else in mind. 'After I find Mandine.'

How could he be thinking about her? It was unlikely she was even there.

But she didn't have time to debate it. She slipped into the safety zone and her senses alerted her to Keily's change in position. With one hand, she swept Jolan around the other side of the lifter, also moving her body into its shadow, while returning with a blast of fire that spat and zinged against the metallic walkways.

To her surprise, she felt the sensation of another attacker. She turned and aimed as a shot went wide of them. Whoever it was, they weren't on the same level as Keily.

Jolan narrowed his eyes. 'Mandine.'

The shot was bad enough that he might be right. But why would she be there at all? Unless she was supposed to be a distraction.

Whatever the case, she had certainly distracted Jolan. He gripped his laser and turned to her. 'Cover me.'

She didn't have time to grab him as her senses alerted her to new action from Keily. She could do nothing other than spray her with fire to keep her pinned down. Damn it! What was he trying to prove? They had only gone to the station to try and get him off-world!

There was nothing she could do about it now. He was out of sight. Her senses told her more or less where he was, but she needed to make sure she distracted Keily from completing her original mission and killing him.

Sensing the sniper was changing her position again, Misilina sprinted out from behind the lifter and dived behind a crate. It was large and spread from the floor to the metal gantry overhead; a much better position and one that meant she could climb up to Keily's level. She needed to end this before she had to come out of the safety zone. Although she had two cans of sugar, the change out while she replenished would leave her vulnerable to attack.

Again sensing movement, Misilina fired more blasts, pleased with the way the high-powered rifle sliced through the metal walkway edges, leaving long burn marks in its wake. No more cowering under superior firepower.

Keily's shots began to rain on her, a constant barrage of

fire trying to keep her pinned down. The safety zone pulled her attention in numerous directions, keeping track of all the incoming shots. She kept returning fire, trying to keep Keily stationary as well. She heaved a breath, wondering if she should come out of the safety zone early to replenish while she had clear cover, but she didn't want to take the risk.

A flare of danger made her dive to the side. To her surprise, Keily stood behind the lifter where she had been with Jolan. But the shots were still coming. They couldn't possibly be Mandine! Was someone else helping them?

But as she began to return fire, Misilina realised the truth. Keily had her weapon—possibly more than one—on auto mode. The firing was targeted at her, but not enough to mean there were eyes behind the sights. Keily had used it to distract her. Misilina cursed herself for not thinking of that.

The weapon cells on the auto guns must have been running out as they began to splutter and die. She took advantage of the distraction to dart to the gantry leading to the next level. She was able to get a clearer shot at Keily there, as the higher position gave her access over the top of the lifter, but her main motivation was to keep the assassin coming after her. As she climbed, she spared a glance over the railing. Their journey in the crate had brought them several levels up, so there was a long network of walkways beneath her, leading from the lowest floor of the station, at least a span below them. It was another way to defeat Keily if it came to hand-to-hand fighting. A fall from that height might be just what she needed to end this.

She hit the assassin with as much fire as she could, happy to see the woman's face pull into a scowl and watch her dart from the lifter to a crate. Misilina jumped up to the next level, feeling shots on her feet as she raced along, Keily firing up at her. Before she reached another control panel and dived behind it, she sent more shots the sniper's way, taking the moment to force herself out of the safety zone and guzzle down some more sugar. She knew she would run out soon. She needed to get some more into her while she had the opportunity.

But now there was only one can left.

Just as she re-entered the zone, she reared back in shock as Keily leapt over the control panel, grabbing her by the throat; the time spent out of the zone had made her too vulnerable. And the assassin knew exactly what to do. The first thing she reached for was the remaining can hanging from Misilina's belt. Keily yanked it off and threw it over the gantry railing.

Now Misilina needed to kill Keily in ten minspans or it was all over.

The woman put a small pistol to Misilina's temple. But Misilina still had the knife. She pulled it out of her belt and thrust it into the sniper's side.

The blade glanced away. She realised, too late, that Keily was wearing something under her jumpsuit, probably a shield skeleton. No knife was going to make a dent in that.

Keily sneered. 'Sorry to disappoint you. Did you think a little rookie like you could beat someone like me?'

Misilina head-butted her, gaining a hold on the weapon. Two pairs of hands fought for the right to wield it.

'How much longer can you hold on?' Keily said. 'Can you really stay in the zone as long as everyone else? You're only a crossbreed. Half of this and half of that. All of nothing.'

Misilina knew better than to let an enemy taunt her into making a mistake, but the words bit. She'd heard them so many times before. She felt the mad desire to prove herself, to stop thinking, to just *react*.

She couldn't take it. It didn't matter if she died. It only mattered that Jolan lived. And to ensure that, Keily had to die. But that didn't mean that Misilina would escape with her life.

She stood up to her full height and the woman came with her, snarling as she continued to struggle for the weapon. But Misilina no longer cared about that. She got a good grip on Keily and threw herself at the gantry railing, trying to dislodge it. She felt it shift behind her. Just a bit more and it would come loose, sending them both tumbling down to the floor so far below. Misilina would use all her strength to make sure Keily hit it hard enough to snap her in half. She knew what it would cost, but it was worth it. It was her job as an agent to ensure the success of her mission.

But Keily figured out what she was trying to do, and as Misilina struck the railing again, hooked her leg around hers, sending them crashing onto the floor. With a flash of triumph, Keily ripped the gun from Misilina's hand. 'A crossbreed could *never* best a purebred. You lose.'

A hand reached out, crossing over Keily's chest, the heel slamming up into the assassin's chin, snapping her head back with a vicious crack. She fell back, stunned, as a shadow passed over Misilina, standing between her and Keily.

It was an agent, if the pink-golden jumpsuit was anything to go by, her body in attack position, her skin the leathery texture of the safety zone. She snarled at Keily, who recovered quickly and raised her weapon. She wasn't fast enough for the agent, who let a broad beam shoot out from her comm unit, turning the sniper's hand red with heat. Keily let out a shriek and dropped the laser as the agent stalked forward, kicking it away and pinning Keily's hand to the ground with her foot.

Keily snapped her other hand around it, trying to push the agent off balance. At first, Misilina thought the sniper had succeeded, as the agent hit the floor, but as they fell, the agent planted her foot on Keily's chest, vaulting the sniper over her head and into the wall. The agent leapt up as Keily did, blocking her strikes and letting loose a combination of punches and kicks into the sniper's torso. Keily buckled and fell to the floor.

As the agent half-turned towards Misilina, she came out of the safety zone. Her furious blue eyes could have bored holes in Keily's skull as she glared down at the fallen assassin.

It was Mother.

Misilina had never seen Mother fight before. She wasn't sure she'd ever seen Mother angry either. She found herself shrinking back as she moved closer, but she shouted a warning as Mother almost turned her back on Keily. Was that her inexperience showing?

But Mother seemed to be enjoying herself. She downed a can of liquid sugar, throwing a spare to Misilina, who'd just come out of the zone herself. 'You know, Keily, I think you'll find that we crossbreeds can hold our own.'

But the sniper rose, her scornful gaze locked on Mother. 'I doubt it. No battle-hardened agent would come out of your safest state mid-fight.' To prove her point, Keily produced a small laser knife from her belt. Her smile was full of foreboding. 'Let's play.'

Mother looked at her hand and sniffed. 'I don't need to play to beat you.' She stretched out her hand just as Father leapt up to join them on the walkway. They locked hands.

Misilina frowned. It looked like they were going to produce energy. But Father couldn't. He hadn't been able to since he'd been injured. Why risk it now?

And Keily knew it. She laughed derisively. 'You can't do that anymore.' She gave Father a mocking look. 'Cripples can't fight any better than crossbreeds.'

Father didn't rise to the bait. His voice was as calm as it was when he was lecturing at the Academy. 'That was over twenty years ago.'

Keily didn't have time to move. Mother raised her right hand, her fingers pointed at the assassin, and streams of light came from her fingertips, throwing Keily back into the wall with a thud and a sizzle as Mother's fiery charge seared her body.

Mother and Father dropped hands, the air still crackling from their energy, and both took another sugar drink. Father wrung his hands a little but otherwise seemed unhurt. He snorted at their fallen foe. 'I think that charge melted your skin to your suit. It will be fun trying to get it off.'

But Mother didn't waste time talking. She went back into the safety zone and, to Misilina's horror, she marched up to Keily, picked her up by the neck and held her over the gantry railing.

This was not the Mother she knew—the compassionate, loving peacemaker. Was she capable of this?

Father was at her side in a flash. 'Sarah, put her down.'

Mother's pinprick eyes looked back at him, her voice a low slur. 'What would Hajitis do?'

Misilina knew they weren't talking about her brother. She watched Keily scrabble her fingers at Mother's hand, her face paling as Mother tightened her grip.

Father's reply was measured and calm. 'You are not Hajitis.'

This seemed to wake Mother up. She pulled the struggling Keily back over the railing and dumped her on the floor at Father's feet. 'Lucky for you,' she sneered at the woman.

'That's enough.' It was the sternest tone Father had ever taken with Mother. But he said no more as she came out of the zone. He put a pair of virtual handcuffs on Keily and pulled her to her feet.

Uncle Pravvit and Aunt Perisina came racing up the stairs. Uncle Pravvit, as usual, had his comm unit in his hands, his finger on the screen. He looked down at Keily. 'So we got her without trouble?'

Mother shrugged. 'Not a problem.' She turned to Misilina and came over to her, putting out her hand to help her up and hugging her. 'Are you okay, darling?'

'Yes, I'm fine.' Misilina couldn't deny she was embarrassed. She was an agent! She didn't need hugging and comforting!

And all this was a sideline to the most important issue. 'Where's Jolan? Did you find him? He went off to get Mandine. We have to save him!'

'It's already done,' Perisina said, her dark eyes pools of calm. 'We found him before we found you.'

'And Mandine?'

Pravvit nodded. 'In custody.'

Misilina looked around frantically, seeking him. She knew it wasn't very agent-like, but she couldn't rest before she knew Jolan was safe.

Then he was running towards her, up the gantry stairs, another squad of agents trailing behind, Mandine in their midst. Jolan raced up to her, his hands on her face. 'Are you all right? She didn't hurt you?'

She smiled. 'I'm fine. Just a few bruises.' Then she couldn't speak, as Jolan's mouth was on hers, kissing her until she fell to the floor, cradled in his arms.

A gasp brought her back to reality and she looked up from Jolan's lips to see her parents staring at them, their eyes wide, their mouths hanging open.

This was not the way to tell them. She knew how hard this was going to be. While her parents were clearly open to Vendel/Verindal relationships, that was different from sanctioning a relationship between their daughter and a member of the high family. While Jolan had played down any resistance to their being a couple, she knew that was likely to be far from reality.

And what if their love led to a bonding? What would her parents think? What would his parents, the leaders of their planet, think? What would be the response from the public? The last time this had happened to a member of the high family it had ended in disaster and bloodshed.

Even Jolan looked chastened as he glanced at her parents' faces, Pravvit and Perisina also blinking in shock. What would they say? Would they forbid it? Surely they wouldn't do that!

'Um, I can explain ...' she finally managed to spit out.

Jolan nodded, shamefaced. 'So can I.'

Her parents seemed to unfreeze as Father looked at Mother, a scowl on his face. 'Damn,' he said. 'I lost the bet.'

Mother shook her head. 'I told you not to make it. Ardon never loses.'

Father's pout would have been comical if Misilina hadn't been reeling. 'What bet?'

'Your father and Uncle Ardon bet on how long it would take the two of you to realise you were perfect for each other,' Mother explained matter-of-factly. 'Ardon said it would be just after you'd graduated, but your father thought you'd have a couple of years as an agent first.'

It was Misilina's turn to freeze. They had bet on this? They had *anticipated* this? 'When did they do that?'

Mother shrugged. 'A couple of years ago, I think. Something like that.' But what about the fact that Jolan was supposed to have bonded with Mandine? They didn't seem too concerned about that. Maybe they'd never believed it would happen.

Jolan sat back on his haunches, but while Misilina felt nothing but numb, he threw his head back and laughed. 'I should have guessed. No wonder he kept telling me to go and see you at the Academy. And he wouldn't hear of me staying away from the awards ceremony. I guess that explains why he was so desperate for me to bring Mandine as well. It makes so much sense now.'

'Speaking of her ...' Mother turned to where the other squad was waiting on the lower level. Father hauled Keily to her feet and marched her down the gantry stairs ahead of them, pushing her into the ring of agents with Mandine.

The former Verindon elite had seen better days. Her shirt was ripped at the shoulder, a bruise blossoming on the skin there. A scrape of blood marred one cheek and one of her eyes was almost swollen shut.

Misilina looked at Jolan. He had done that? It was further than she'd expected him to go. But as she watched the agents snarl at her, she wondered if all the damage was Jolan's.

Mandine didn't seem all that worried if the rage on her face was anything to go by. She looked back and forth between Jolan and Misilina and her eyes snapped with scorn. 'Seriously? You're replacing me with *her*? A crossbreed?'

Mother stiffened and Father put a hand on her arm. But they didn't need to say anything as Jolan curled his lip. 'Yeah well, she's not likely to kill me, is she? And unlike you, she could if she wanted to. She doesn't need to hire someone to do her dirty work.'

Misilina's agent side puffed up with pride, but something in her wasn't sure it was the best way to describe the one you loved. But she was an agent first, and so were most of the people around her, who nodded and murmured their agreement. Pravvit winked at her.

Every agent tensed as a bustle of noise came along the gangway. Soon, Misilina could see a group of Tekkon crowd control, heavily armed, scowls on their faces. Ambassador Utreysin was leading them. She looked at Jolan. Would they try to arrest them? If Mandine and Keily's faces were any indication, that was what they expected.

Father's eyes hardened. 'Here we go.'

Mother hefted her comm unit, the gun function active, along with her translator. 'Let me deal with them.'

Mother was going to deal with them? Surely Father was the senior agent.

As the group approached, Ambassador Utreysin held his arms out. 'My fellow Verindonians, I see you have apprehended the vicious Mandine in the middle of her attempt to kill Lord Jolan.'

'You ...' spat Mandine. 'How dare you?'

The ambassador smiled at Mother. 'Agent Sarah! I'm happy you were able to take care of this without too much trouble and especially before harm was done.'

'Yes, we did indeed, Ambassador. Despite your best efforts, we saved Jolan's life.'

A combination of fear and rage passed across Utreysin's face. 'What?'

'Don't try and deny it. Remember, I can tell when you're lying. Not that I need that. We're fully aware of what you did. Evidently, you weren't happy having to stay on Darsair for so long. And you won't be here much longer. You'll be returning to Verindon to stand trial for conspiracy to murder a member of the Verindonian High Family.'

'I-I-I did no such—'

Lie. Mother clearly heard it too. 'Why even bother with that, Ambassador?'

But he wasn't giving up. 'You can't do anything to me. These men with me, these loyal Tekkon guards, know my innocence.' He turned to the crowd control with him. 'Arrest them!'

Given there were only twenty guards and they were facing twenty armed Vendel, it was a wonder he bothered to try. Maybe he planned to sneak away during their fight.

But Mother marched up to the leader, pushing his weapon out of the way and waved her credentials tag in his face. The man's angular face looked affronted and he pressed his automatic translator and immediately began to babble. 'You are to be arrested for aiding and abetting a man who took part in a rebellion. That man,' he pointed at Jolan, 'incited rebels to destroy a factory. Such an offence is punishable by death on our planet.'

The smug look was back on Mandine's face. 'Yes, Jolan. You really shouldn't have done that. I knew you had trouble controlling your impulses, but ...'

Mother held up her hand. 'Not so fast.' She peered at the insignia on the Darsairian's chest. 'Officer L'ssanne, is it?'

L'ssanne looked confused, but responded with a snort before trying to push his way past her.

'Officer L'ssanne, we are here with the permission of the Darsairian Chief Government—'

'This is *Tekkon*,' the man snapped. 'Our government has sovereignty unless members of the chief government are present.'

'Unless a state of control has been declared,' said Mother patiently. 'And given the corruption that has been uncovered in the upper echelons of the Tekkon government, it has.'

As she spoke, another squad of troops appeared, also Darsairian, but with different insignia on their uniforms. Utreysin, L'ssanne and his force looked around. 'What is this?'

'We have supplied the Darsairian Chief Government with evidence that the Tekkon government conspired with two *former* Verindonian elites,' Mother seemed to take great delight in stressing that word as she glanced at Utreysin and Mandine, 'to incite a rebellion in their city as a cover to aid in the assassination of a member of the Verindonian High Family.'

L'ssanne's face paled to a lighter grey. 'What?'

Pravvit stepped forward, holding out his comm unit. 'We discovered some highly classified documents from the Icho Company, which also implicated several members of the Tekkon government, not to mention a number of the Tekkon crowd control force. These documents were passed between you, Ambassador Utreysin, and Lady Mandine and her father.'

Mother looked at what Pravvit held out. 'And it seems your name is on it, officer.'

L'ssanne looked alarmed as he and his force were surrounded by the Darsairian troops. 'This … this is an outrage!'

'Hear how low his voice is, Misilina?' Father said beside her, loud enough for all to hear. 'What does that mean in a Darsairian?'

'A lie,' she confirmed.

He nodded. 'And I'm sure your mother can confirm that.'

But before Mother could, Misilina spoke up. 'So can I. He's definitely lying.'

Again, she was the focus of attention, as every Verindonian apart from Jolan stared at her.

Mother's face became like a ray of light. 'Misilina, can you lie detect?'

There was no need to congratulate herself on developing a talent she should have had when she was ten. 'It seems I can.'

For a moment, she thought Mother was going to dive on her for another hug. Fortunately, she dragged her eyes away and turned her attention back to the troops who were arresting L'ssanne and his men. 'I can indeed confirm that he is lying. The evidence of his betrayal, as well as the government's, has already been given to the Darsairian Chief Government. Take him away.'

The troops surrounded L'ssanne's force and made a barking noise at them, prodding them with electrified sticks, as they led them away. Jolan frowned. 'That's odd.'

'That's the way they treat traitors amongst their people,' said Misilina. She looked at Pravvit. 'There's really evidence that they were in on all this?'

'Oh yes,' he said, holding up his comm unit and showing her a small screen of what looked like a much larger dossier. 'Plenty of it.' He looked at Mandine. 'Next time you conspire against your leaders, get better security.'

'There won't be a next time,' said Father tersely.

Mandine's bottom lip began trembling as her eyes filled with tears. 'But they coerced me into it. They threatened me!'

Lie, lie, lie.

Mother didn't even flinch. 'Do you really think we're going to believe that?' She glanced at Misilina. 'You got that as well?'

'Oh yes, it was obvious.'

'We'll have to do some tests when we get home to see exactly how far your ability extends.' Mother gave Mandine a scathing look. 'These lies are a bit too blatant to tell us that.'

But the disgraced elite still wouldn't give up. 'It was Keily! It was her idea.'

The assassin fixed her furious gaze on Mandine. 'Don't you *dare* try and pin this on me.' She turned a sullen eye to Keridan. 'I can tell you all she did. I'm more than willing to cooperate.'

Mandine's face morphed from tragedy to rage. '*You* will say nothing. You were supposed to be the best! You *told* me you were the best! You can't even shoot straight.'

Keridan ignored Mandine and glanced at the assassin. 'Whether you talk or not makes no difference to us. It will also make no difference to *you*.' He gestured to the squad of agents. 'Take them to the prison ship and secure them.'

Keily took his pronouncement quietly but Utreysin and Mandine were far less subdued. One shouted pleas of innocence and the other shrieks of rage. They continued to reverberate throughout the docking station for a few minspans.

'We have a prison ship here?' Misilina asked.

'Just a converted Star Runner,' said Aunt Perisina. 'It was the best we could do at short notice.'

'But it was enough,' Father said. He looked between Misilina and Jolan. 'Well, let's get you home. I need to pay up.'

Mother stopped him. 'We need to take leave of the Darsairian government envoys first. This way. I also need to make sure they've retrieved the bodies of our fallen.'

Her words turned Misilina cold. Had they lost everyone? 'Mother, Tenya, Amatara and Dina, are they …? Did they …?'

Sorrow filled Mother's face. 'You didn't know? You knew about the boys, right?' Missy nodded. 'I'm sorry, they all died. We have space set aside to return them so they can be delivered back to their families for passing services.'

'Did they find Enyi?' Misilina couldn't return without her.

'Yes,' Mother said. 'Her body was retrieved as well. The Darsarian Chief Government was keen to do all they could to help us once we sent them proof of the plot to kill Jolan.'

Misilina blinked the tears back. It was just as she'd feared. At least they would be remembered with honour.

They marched back the way they'd come, this time walking beside the conveyor belt, which still trundled innocuous crates and boxes towards multiple destinations. Misilina wondered what they held. Hopefully, no rebels. It would cause a huge incident and that was the last thing they needed.

Once they reached the entrance to the docking station, Mother had a few words with the workers milling around. After a brief wait, they were told to exit.

To Misilina's surprise, an awning decorated with official Darsairian cube insignias had been erected near the entryway. An obsequious Darsairian raced up to Mother, speaking so fast Misilina couldn't pick up what he said and wasn't sure the translator had either. But Mother was unruffled. She replied in Darsairian!

Missy felt her mouth drop open. 'When did Mother learn to speak their language?'

Father smiled. 'She's gained a good understanding of a number of languages from the surrounding planets. She doesn't often get a chance to use them, but she doesn't mind Darsairian. She says it's easier than Verindonian.'

It had never occurred to Misilina that her mother, rather than her father, would be the leader here. He was a great agent; had always been a great agent. Mother was ...

A crossbreed. An outsider. Just like her.

She felt shame wash over her. She had already realised she thought this way, so it shouldn't have been such a shock, but she hadn't expected her prejudice to be so starkly demonstrated.

Jolan curled his hand around hers. He stepped back as she jumped. 'Just saying hello.' He kissed her on the cheek.

She smiled at him before turning back to the scene before her. 'Did you know she could do all that?'

He shrugged. 'I knew Father relied on her a lot for interplanetary relations. I didn't know she was keen on languages, though. I guess she figured she'd learnt one, why not others?'

His smile didn't disarm her. 'How could I have misjudged her?' She lowered her voice so Father couldn't hear.

Jolan's face grew serious. 'So you missed some things. You can't know everything about everybody.'

'But she's my *mother*!'

He seemed intrigued by her embarrassment. 'Well, it's not like you can't make it up to her. Plenty of time for that.'

He was right, she realised, as Mother waved the two of them

over. The Darsairian dignitary bowed before him and uttered some apologies in broken Verindonian, with additional supplications made in Darsairian and translated. The Darsairian then waved them towards some refreshments their servants were hurrying to prepare.

Misilina's stomach growled and Jolan took a step forward, but Mother held out her hand. 'No.' She turned back to the official. 'We can no longer delay our departure. We must leave Darsair and return to Verindon.'

The official pleaded a bit longer, but Mother remained unmoved. Begrudgingly, the man nodded.

Mother smiled. 'Then we will take our leave.' She held her fists together and bowed over them, as Darsairian protocol dictated, and everyone copied her. The Darsairians returned the gesture, even the docking station workers.

'We're done here,' Mother said to Father. 'Let's go.'

They turned and re-entered the station, walking quickly towards landing bay forty-nine, where their Star Runner was docked. This time they took an official route through passenger lifters and moving walkways, guided by a docking station attendant.

Misilina found herself beside her mother. She had to say something. 'I didn't know you could do all that.'

'Do what?'

'Talk to Darsairians.'

She laughed. 'It's just another language.'

'But all the protocols and everything.'

'It's what I do.'

Yes, it was. And Misilina had ignored it. The guilt and shame of it hit her again.

She stopped walking and turned to her mother. 'I'm sorry.'

'What for?' But she sensed Mother already knew.

'I … I …' *I'm sorry for selling you short. I'm sorry for being a hypocrite. I'm sorry for not appreciating you.*

Was Mother also a mind-reader? Because Missy didn't say all that, but her mother's face looked brighter than it had for a long time. It reminded her of the carefree days of her childhood before Missy had been weighed down with agent responsibilities and considerations. Mother had just been Mother then.

She put a hand on Missy's shoulder. 'Let's go home.'

But Misilina had one more thing to clear up. 'Father?'

'Yes, darling?'

'How long have you been able to produce energy with Mother?'

The scars pulled across his face as he grinned. 'A few years now. It's been coming back gradually over the past ten years or so. It was a bit painful at first and I still can't do it much, but it worked today.'

'Thankfully,' Mother said with a smile.

'Are you three coming?' said Uncle Pravvit. They hurried to catch up.

It was time they left Darsair and Misilina wasn't sure she ever wanted to see its dark sky again. She longed for the colours of Verindon.

CHAPTER NINETEEN

'But my Lord, you know what the public will think of this!'

Councillor Klager seemed to revel in his portents of doom. The councillor was from the old line and was one of the few that Uncle Ardon had left in his cabinet in the new order. He had seemed more progressive than the others.

But not *that* progressive. His cloudy blue eyes peered at Misilina as though she had disgraced herself in the throne room, turning back to Ardon and Talma, where they sat on their thrones.

Despite her parents' immediate acceptance of her relationship with Jolan, Misilina knew they had expected this reaction. She'd discussed it with them. They stood to the side, Mother with her arms folded, Father watching Klager carefully.

Misilina adjusted the rainbow-coloured mourning band on her wrist. They'd held the passing services for the fallen agents a few days earlier, and every agent would wear the bands for the next week. It would be hard taking it off at all, and the councillor's mutterings were getting on her nerves more than she would have thought. She'd asked if they could wait until the week of remembrance was over before they did this, but the council had been in an uproar when news of the relationship had reached them, so Ardon had begrudgingly agreed to discuss it as soon as possible.

Jolan had said he would be here for this, but he hadn't turned up yet. Misilina turned again to the throne room's ornate lukis-encrusted door, but it remained closed. She needed his support given all the councillors were eyeing her, some with suspicion, some with thoughtful expressions. She wondered what they were pondering—a way that this could work or a way that they could tactfully tell Ardon it never would?

Of all the council members, only High Commander Zaden seemed truly accepting. He hadn't looked shocked when he'd heard, but had instantly entered into talks with Father about how they handled this. Like they had planned for this eventuality. It made Misilina cringe to think just how many people *had* expected this.

She looked again at the man she hoped would be her future father-in-law. As usual, he seemed unruffled, almost bored. He leant his chin on one hand, propping up his elbow on the arm of his throne. 'Yes, I'm sure the public will have a great deal to say. Of course, I don't think it's going to be as gloomy as you're suggesting.'

'Perhaps,' said Aunt Talma, speaking tentatively, 'we need to take this to the people to see what their response will be.'

Klager dismissed that notion with a wave of his hand. 'We know what the response will be. The last time an agent,' again he looked down his nose at Misilina, 'bonded with a member of the high family, it ended in the death of the Verindal leader and a huge battle that cost many lives and resulted in a wedge being driven between Verindal and Vendel for hundreds of years, one only recently overcome.' He gave a half-smile to Mother and Father, who didn't return it. 'While the bonding of two agents, one with some Verindal blood, was allowed, even then it was a while before Agent Sarah was accepted.'

'By the council, certainly,' Mother said, an edge to her voice. 'The public was much quicker to do so.'

Klager's back stiffened. 'That's not how I remember it.'

'I'm sure,' muttered Ardon. 'However, I remember it well, and I know Agent Sarah is right. Certainly, it wasn't immediate, but she was accepted and has become a clear asset in our interplanetary relations. This is only a step further.'

'A monumental one, my Lord!' Klager blustered. 'To put a

crossbreed on the throne—'

Father's eyes flashed. 'Be careful, councillor.'

Klager turned his pompous gaze on Father. '*You* be careful, Agent Keridan. I'm sure you would have a vested interest in—'

Mother moved forward, fury in her eyes. Father stopped her.

Ardon held up his hands. 'Councillor, how likely is it that my youngest child will end up on the throne? I have two other boys and a girl. They're all in the line of succession before Lord Jolan. The chances that he will end up reigning are minuscule.'

'But still there, my Lord. And we all know how *accidents* can happen.'

Both Mother and Father stepped closer this time and the councillor took a quick step back. But it was Ardon who rose from his throne and towered over Klager. 'Councillor, that is out of line. The only thing you've demonstrated is how your prejudice is still alive and well. I had thought better of you.'

Klager's face paled. He must have realised he'd gone too far. 'But my Lord, I am only speaking as the public will speak. This is what *they* will say. We can talk about the good character of these agents as much as we like, but it will make no difference if the public takes exception to the relationship, as they are likely to do!'

'Oh, are they?' Jolan said.

Everyone turned as he entered, his guard trailing him. He'd opened the door himself, which is why the door guards took a moment to announce him.

Klager and the other councillors bowed to him, as did Mother and Father. Misilina did as well, although he'd told her not to, but she didn't want to be seen as some kind of upstart who was trying to take advantage of him, especially after what had happened with Mandine. She watched him carefully to see how he'd react.

He didn't notice. He was too busy looking at the comm watch on his wrist.

Ardon raised an eyebrow. 'Jolan?'

He looked up. 'Sorry, Father. Just getting things sorted.' He turned to the councillor. 'I think our people are more than ready for this. It's been over twenty years since Sarah and Keridan were bonded and there's been every acceptance of them as a couple.'

Klager puffed himself up. 'Not amongst *us* there hasn't been.'

Too late, he realised what he'd said. Father narrowed his eyes and Ardon leant forward on the arm of his throne. 'And who exactly are "us", councillor?'

Klager's face paled. 'I was speaking of the people.'

'Really?' said Jolan. 'I think they might be of a different mind.'

He turned his wrist comm to the wall and beamed a feed onto it. On it were several people Misilina thought she recognised. She didn't follow celebrities on the comm channels much. She'd been too busy graduating as an agent. But here were a group of them having an animated conversation. Jolan increased the volume.

'... no reason why Lord Jolan shouldn't bond with an agent if he chooses to,' one said. Misilina frowned. Wasn't it Zena? She was a high-profile comm star with millions of followers. 'I mean, he's a nice guy and deserves to be happy with whoever he chooses.'

'Especially since he already chose an elite only to have her betray him in the worst possible way.' That was Muxir, another influential figure on the channels.

'Why are we still listening to our out-of-date leaders when it comes to who we bond with anyway? No one wants this kind of restriction anymore, clearly even at the top,' said Dimiso, who was the highest-profile influencer of the lot. Even Misilina had tuned in for some of his features. 'So why won't our leadership listen to one of us? And Jolan *is* one of us. He represents the future of our planet, not the old ways.'

Jolan then increased the feed to show how many people were watching them. It was well over twenty million. And there were another ten million who'd watched earlier. All bound to be young, all people who listened to these three more than anyone in elite circles.

'And if they allow this, it would mean so much to so many,' said Zena, sitting back. 'I know of at least six other couples amongst the elite who want to bond with Vendel. And why not do it? Ander is desperate to bond with ... who was that agent?'

Klager spluttered. 'Ander? They don't mean ... *my son?*'

'Sorry,' said Jolan with an innocent blink. 'Did I forget to mention that?'

'My son is in love with an agent?' The old man threw up his hands.

Ardon put a hand to his mouth and Misilina could see his shoulders shaking. 'Perhaps you need to rethink your objections, councillor.'

Klager went over to his fellow councillors and Missy heard angry hissing as the men and women debated this latest development. Only High Commander Zaden didn't participate.

Jolan turned to his parents. 'Seriously, Father, there is so much support for this, admittedly not from the older members of the population, but the young ones. People our age.' He took Missy's hand. 'They're the first generation of Verindal in ... I don't know how long, who've made friends with agents and spent time with them. Some of them have developed relationships. How can we keep them apart?'

Ardon chuckled. 'How can we indeed, son? Well, you've got our support.' He and Talma smiled at Misilina. She looked at her parents, who were holding hands and looking delighted.

She bent her head towards Jolan. 'How did you find out about this?'

'Oh, someone reached out.'

Lie. Why would he be lying about that? 'Jolan, that's not true.'

He looked crestfallen. 'Damn it. I forgot you could do that now.'

Uncertainty filled her. What possible reason did he have to lie about this? 'Please tell me the truth.'

He looked down, shamefaced. 'To be honest, I started talking to people like Zena and Dimiso a while ago. I thought this might be a cause they could get behind.'

She folded her arms. There was more. 'Why?'

He coughed. 'I thought it could come in useful sometime.'

There was still more. She raised an eyebrow and waited.

His shoulders sagged. 'Fine. I knew I'd probably never get you, but I had to do everything I could just in *case* something happened between us. And even if it didn't, I knew there might be another couple ...'

She felt her mouth drop open. 'You did this for me?'

There was hope in his eyes. 'Yes.'

'How long?'

'What?'

'How long ago did you start work on this?'

The guilty look was back. 'A few of years ago now.'

Misilina reeled. He couldn't be serious! He had been laying the groundwork for a potential relationship between them for years! Her parents and his had been betting on it! And she'd kept her head down, studying to be an agent, watching him strut past with a never-ending stream of women.

'You dated a lot,' she said flatly.

He sighed and rubbed the back of his neck. 'You know that was expected. And as I said, I never thought I had a chance with you. Well, not much of one. I'd sort of given up when I agreed to bond with Mandine.'

'But what about all those other girls? Did you have to lead them on like that?' How many had there been? That parade of starry-eyed empty heads would have been wishing he would just say the word ...

But what had she called those women? Empty-headed. Gold diggers. Mercenary. She hadn't thought they'd deserved him and didn't know why he'd spent his time with them. She'd despised him for it.

So was she any better? She would have thought less of him if he'd chosen one, just as she had with Mandine.

She took his hands. 'Promise me no more of that.'

'No more other girls?' he said, putting his arms around her. 'Easy.'

'No more lying.'

He laughed. 'I can't get away with that anyway, so sure thing. And maybe you can promise something in return.'

'What's that?'

'A little less work? A little more time for fun? Like you used to do.'

She looked at him. Was there anything she wouldn't do for him now? 'On one condition.'

'What?'

'Don't set my hair on fire.'

He laughed again. 'Never.' And he kissed her.